I0212261

# The Integration of Faith and Learning among Collegiate Theatre Artists

# A Hermeneutical Phenomenological Study

# The Integration of Faith and Learning among Collegiate Theatre Artists

## A Hermeneutical Phenomenological Study

### Jeffrey W. Tirrell

CLAREMONT DISSERTATIONS
OF DISTINCTION

The Integration of Faith and Learning among Collegiate Theatre Artists
A Hermeneutical Phenomenological Study
©2018 Claremont Press
1325 N. College Ave
Claremont, CA 91711

ISBN 9781946230072

Library of Congress Cataloging-in-Publication Data

The Integration of Faith and Learning among Collegiate Theatre Artists
A Hermeneutical Phenomenological Study / Jeffrey W. Tirrell

     xiii+137 Pp. 15x22cm. –(Claremont Dissertations of
     Distinction 1)
     Includes bibliographical references and index.
     ISBN 9781946230072
     Subjects: 1. Theater – Religious aspects – Christianity.
     2. Religion and Drama. 3. Edmund Husserl, 1859-1938.

     Call Number: PN 2049 T57 2018a

Cover Credit: Michaelkensy.de

# Table of Contents

## *Preface*

Since the early days of Christianity there has been a contentious relationship between the theatre and the pulpit, with each vying for the hearts and minds of their respective audience. Especially in the United States, this contention has often led to excommunication of known theatre practitioners by churches, and the creation of plays mocking Christians or church practices by those who found no welcome within church walls. But as technology has improved and the world has grown more and more interconnected, and particularly because of the advent of film and its ability to tell stories to a multitude of audiences, many within Christianity have begun to explore how theatre, film, and other arts might enhance, enlighten, or explain their faith.

The literature surrounding the intersection of Christianity and theatre is scarce, usually focusing on how theatrical conventions can be used within the church; there is very little that aims to understand Christian theatre professionals on their own terms. In an attempt to start addressing this dearth of material and research, this study investigates how one population of Christian theatre students and faculty at a faith-based, Christian university perceive and imagine faith integration happening within their department. The following question was asked: How do both students and faculty within theatre departments at faith-based Christian colleges and universities imagine faith integration and spiritual growth to occur within their departments? In tandem with this question comes a second: What is the perceived faith integration and spiritual growth by these same undergraduates, and what is the intended faith integration and spiritual growth presented by the faculty who teach within the major?

Using a hermeneutical phenomenological framework, the researcher conducted in-person interviews with a sample of current theatre students, alumni/ae, and the full-time departmental faculty in order to better understand how faith integration was understood in their context. Data was then coded and examined for patterns that might provide insight into how these questions could be answered. From this data it was concluded that faculty viewed both the ideal and the perception of faith integration through the lens of their instructional material and their personal motivations, and students demonstrated that faculty modeling of the integration of faith and learning was the most perceived method within their department, as well as the ideal way for it to occur. Students also presented a far more balanced perception of faith integration than their faculty counterparts.

It is hoped that this study will build upon a previous study that examined the integration of faith and learning within a general, faith-based collegiate population, and that it can be replicated at other schools to examine its transferability and application. The purpose of such a study is to provide new insights into how students understand the integration of faith and learning, with the intention that these insights might inform the way faculty choose to teach their areas within theatrical studies. This is important for the Church and practical theologians because it can shed light on where artists view the integration of faith in their craft and how that faith is expressed, which can in turn lead to potentially new ways for understanding and communicating the gospel.

# Introduction

John Cochran was a working black actor in the 60s, in television. Get the picture, he was that good. And [he] didn't find fulfillment in the industry that he thought he would as a storyteller. He ended up going to Yale and running that department for a while. Didn't find the fulfillment in Yale drama, the School of Drama, that he thought he would. Ended up marrying a grad student who was Christian, so then he converted. The first thing he wanted to do was go see a church play that he'd seen advertised because he's like, "I finally get it, I know where the connection is, I know what I've been missing! I cannot wait to see where it's really happening!" So he showed up early because he thought it would be crowded, because he thought the work would be so good and so life changing. And sat in the front row. He said his heart was racing, he felt like a 6-yearold. Well, the thing started, and we do what we do, or did in the [19]80s anyway. And so it was dreadful. And at the end of it, he put his head in his hands and started crying. And an usher came up to him, thinking he'd been, you know, moved by the story, and asked if he could help him. And because he didn't know how to behave in church [John] grabbed his arm and said to him, "What's happened here?" And [the usher] said, "What do you mean?" And the question [John] asked was not, "Are these people artists?" "Or trained?" or whatever. He asked him, "Aren't these people Christians?" Because the work was so bad he questioned their salvation.

The above story is heartbreaking, all the more so because it is true. It was relayed during an interview with one of the faculty who participated in this study, and captures the heart of why this study was undertaken. The Theatre and the Church have nearly always had an uneasy relationship, full of mutual distrust, appropriation, and at times vitriolic condemnation. Conservative Christians in particular have a long history of separation from theaters, a place described as the devil's "Church."[1] But in the entertainment-driven climate of Southern California, and in a postmodern era where stories compete not only for the attention but the "truthfulness" of how something is remembered, many Christians increasingly

---

[1] "But if it be in our conscience, that God abhors, that he detests, that God is offended as the Devil is fed by Theaters; how say we that we worship God in his Church, which serve the Devil always at plays, and that wittingly, and willingly?" Quoted from Anthony Munday, the author of the *Third Blast of Retrait from Plaies and Theaters*, 1580, drawing from Salvian of Marseilles (ca. 400–480 AD). This sentiment was not unique. The Reverend Richard Baxter, an English Puritan pastor in the mid-1600s, wrote that "the Devil hath apishly made these [theaters] his Churches, in competition with the Churches of Christ." Quotations from William Orme, *The Practical Works of the Rev. Richard Baxter, With a Life of the Author and a Critical Examination of His Writings* (London: Mills, Jowett and Mills, 1830), 5:485.

1

believe that it is more important than ever to engage with the narrative arts so that the Christian message, which claims access to Ultimate Truth, can be heard and demonstrated through the mouths and works of Christ's followers.

Because of this, many Christian colleges and universities—particularly in larger, urban areas—now offer degrees in theatre or film, two art forms that carry social clout in a media-saturated culture. While many of these programs initially lagged behind in technology and proper training compared to state universities and private secular institutions, today several top-tier evangelical universities boast well-respected theatre and/or film departments, and Fuller Theological Seminary (perhaps the most well-known and respected evangelical seminary in the United States) has devoted considerable resources toward developing the Brehm Center, "a spiritually nurturing community that guides and resources Christian leaders to critically engage culture, explore their calling, and creatively integrate worship, theology, and the arts."[2] Thus the evangelical Christian community, at least in the greater Los Angeles area, is seeking after more constructive engagement with the entertainment industry than has existed in years past.[3]

But while this is all well and good (and indeed necessary), the underlying issues that arise from this story have as much to do with technical training as they do with spiritual awareness. Which brings us back to this study. Having witnessed dozens of plays, short films, and other artistic expressions from undergraduate theatre and film students over the years, this author has little doubt that students are being well trained in all elements of theatrical acting, filmmaking, and story development. But any student from UCLA or USC can claim just as much. What is stated to set these departments apart from their secular counterparts is that there is a faith-based component that pervades the instruction, a component that "seek[s] to advance the work of God in the world."[4] But how do students, and particularly theatre students, perceive the faith element within their studies? And further, since many of them are Christians themselves, how do they want faith integration to happen in their work? How do they imagine it?

This study seeks to discover two different pieces of information, from two different perspectives: first, how do students imagine the ideal integration of faith and learning (IFL) within their academic pursuits, and how do they actually perceive it happening?; and second, how do the faculty who teach these students imagine the ideal IFL, and how do they actually perceive it happening? Similar studies have been done in the past with general undergraduate Christian students, as will be discussed in chapter one, but it is the desire of this study to limit the population of

---

[2] As found on the Brehm Center website, accessed 1 September, 2015, https://web.archive.org/web/20160217214402. In the greater Los Angeles area, the three largest evangelical Christian universities (Azusa Pacific University, Biola University, and California Baptist University) all offer degrees in theatre and in cinema/film.

[3] For a brief history of Christian engagement in Hollywood, see chapter 2, "A Brief History of the Church and Hollywood," of Robert K. Johnston, *Reel Spirituality: Theology and Film in Dialogue* (2nd ed.; Grand Rapids, MI: Baker Academic, 2006), 41–53.

[4] As found in the Azusa Pacific University "Mission Statement," accessed September 1, 2015, https://web.archive.org/ web/ 20151003 040330.

students and faculty to those who study and teach theatre arts, specifically within a Christian university context.

The aim or purpose of this study is to fill in a literary gap in the research related to theatrical studies. While much has been written from the perspective of theologians examining theatrical appropriation in ecclesiastical settings, very little has been written by or for theatrical professionals relating to Christian faith formation. This omission affects not only the field of theatrical studies but also all fields that seek to engage with the performing arts, including practical theology. Thus, this type of study has great relevance for those interested in an interdisciplinary engagement that crosses theological-theatrical borders. From the perspective of the educational arts communities, it can allow similar institutions to hear firsthand from faculty and students who are similar to their own populations about how they are faring in attempts to engage in faith integration, which in turn may allow these institutions to learn from the successes and/or weaknesses that arose from the data. From the perspective of practical theologians, this study can be valuable because it can provide a glimpse into how future professional (and potential ecclesiastical) artists are thinking about their faith and their craft now, as well as a subsequent inference about how this understanding will impact the values, morals, and perspectives portrayed in their created art once they enter into churches and the larger entertainment culture. It is hoped that the wider Church will see future artists engaging in strong critical reflection on the practices of their faith, the practices of the Church, and the practices of the world, which is very much in the heart of the definition of practical theology put forth by Swinton and Mowat in their book *Practical Theology and Qualitative Research*.[5]

The approach of this study will be a hermeneutical phenomenology. Phenomenology, first popularized by Edmund Husserl, is a qualitative methodology that seeks to understand and explain the experiences of those who encounter or participate in a particular phenomenon. A *hermeneutical* phenomenology takes it one step further and attempts not only to explain the phenomenon but also to interpret it. By approaching the subject of faith integration this way it will free up the data not only to speak on its own terms but also to be critiqued for its effectiveness, thus allowing for constructive suggestions and possible adaptation to other similar fields of study.

This study initially evolved from the author's own experiences as a student of theatre at a Christian university, where there seemed to be very little interaction between personal faith and theatrical studies. The two fields seemed distant and unrelated; intellectually, it was known that God was in the arts and that the arts were a way of glorifying God, but that knowledge did not translate into visible action. With the benefit of hindsight, after college the author began to see this disconnect more clearly and wondered if others had also experienced it. Thus, the desire to study the narrative arts and theology in tandem began to emerge and since has manifested itself in a clearer desire to study how faith integration is occurring (or

---

[5] John Swinton and Harriet Mowat, *Practical Theology and Qualitative Research* (London: SCM Press, 2006), 6.

even *if* it is occurring) in the current curriculums and created experiences of student Christian artists today.

This study has personal significance for many reasons. Having been involved in live theatre for the better part of twenty years, and having seen the powerful impact it can have on people, the author has noted experiences and perceptions that people are far more likely to change their attitude or behavior toward something (or someone) if they have a strong emotional reaction to it; simply trying to logically or empirically prove or disprove the point rarely produces the same affective change. Within the world of biblical academics it was discovered that much of the material used was rather dry and "lifeless" when compared to the vivacity of a well-written script; though it was well reasoned, it did not hold sway over the imagination in the same way that a powerfully told film or theatrical piece could. There appeared to be something about the human condition that associates emotional response with mental assent or dissent. Thus, it seemed only logical that there were things that artists could teach theologians.

Conversely, theologians could also teach artists about the wisdom, insights, and nuances that are required to tell the Christian story (or even a Christian virtue) faithfully. Many artists tend to sacrifice those kinds of details for the larger story, which can be dangerous when dealing with religious or theological material. Thus the training up of artists to think about philosophical assumptions, worldviews, and historical understandings about God, Jesus, heaven, etc., can be exceedingly helpful in creating work that is faithful to what the artist or artistic community actually believes. Having lived in both worlds (the world of biblical scholarship and the world of performing arts), the author believes that keeping these two fields in dialogue is extremely important for their growth and maturation.

A second reason this study is personally significant is because of the disconnect between faith and artistic endeavors mentioned above. The atmosphere of the theatre created a false dichotomy between the *sacred*, i.e., chapel services, bible classes, church, etc., and the *secular*, i.e., theatre classes and productions. While this dichotomy is not believed by the author to be real, or that it was intentionally created by the department, it nonetheless led to questions: Have students or faculty thought about how to integrate what a person believes and what they do? Is there a way to pay more than lip service to a person's faith and their art? Is praying before a performance or a rehearsal the only way to integrate faith and art? What is covered in core classes for other students getting similar degrees? Are they trained to think critically about their faith and their art, or are they taught only the techniques and skills that are learned in any state or public school in the country? While this particular study does not seek to answer all of these questions, it is the first step in a lifelong journey to explore them more fully.

The third and final reason this study is personally significant is because of a long-held desire to know the way that both current faculty and current theatre students understand their faith. It is the author's intention to teach undergraduate students who want to work in (or at least engage with) the arts, and specifically students at a Christian university. It is hoped that having training in the fields of practical theology and biblical studies will allow for better understanding of the fundamental assumptions that students bring to their faith as it relates to their desired

4

profession. Just as a doctor needs to know the different veins within the body, so this training has grown and developed knowledge about the different denominations, teachings, and histories within the Christian body. This knowledge, combined with the knowledge of how today's student artists understand their faith and envision it intersecting with their work, will allow for better teaching and mentoring by providing more personalized and relevant instruction.

As with any research project, there are strengths and limitations to what has been done here. An obvious strength lies in the fact that, as far as the author can find, no study has been undertaken which examines the integration of faith and theatre at a Christian college or university. Nor has there been a study which examines theatre faculty instruction of spiritual matters, student perceptions of faith integration in the narrative arts, or the faculty's and students' visions for IFL. This is new territory. The spirituality of artists can be tricky to quantify because of the emotional impetus required for the craft. Thus, creating a qualitative study which examines both the *imagined vision* for IFL and the *perceived* IFL from both the student and the faculty points of view is vital. It not only fills a hole in the literature but is an invaluable resource for arts instructors who desire to shape student artists to understand their faith and use it wisely in their work. It allows these teachers to see what students are actually learning from their classes and instruction, to set goals based on their vision for IFL in their classes and productions, and (if necessary) to modify their methods to improve the quality of their training.

The limitations of this study are many, but the key limitations are: first, that it is only studying undergraduate theatre majors and faculty, and does not address students studying other disciplines or those at different levels of education. It also is geographically limited to Southern California and does not take into account geocultural differences at Christian universities in other places around the country. Finally, this study is limited in that it does not examine spirituality within the larger context of public and secular private institutions, nor does it examine spirituality from faith traditions other than Christianity.

After these preliminary comments, which have hopefully provided a sense of what this study is about, why it is being done, and what it hopes to learn, chapter one will provide an overview of the relevant literature related to the subjects at hand. Because this study is interdisciplinary in nature, literature will be examined from several different fields. From the realm of "Christian faith," appropriate literature will be discussed from the disciplines of religious education (specifically evangelical understandings of Christian education); spiritual formation; and the limited, relevant literature that is specific to the subject of faith integration in Christian colleges and universities. Then, appropriate literature from the realm of theatrical studies will be discussed from the disciplines of theatre education, spirituality within theatre, and Christianity and theatre.

Once the literary base has been established for the study, chapter two will describe the research project in more detail. With a focus on methodology, more information about hermeneutical phenomenology will be provided. This will support the rationale for the study. From there, a point-by-point examination of the criteria for the study will be given, including who was involved; at what type of institution the study took place (the name of the institution is not given due to promised anonymity); how the data was collected; and how the data was processed, coded, and analyzed.

After the necessary preliminary information has been disseminated, chapters three and four will move into the actual findings of the study: What did students imagine to be the ideal forms, expressions, and methods for integrating faith and learning? What did faculty imagine? Further, how did students perceive the integration of faith and learning within their theatrical studies? And how did faculty perceive it? The answers to these four questions will appear in these chapters through the particular, detailed responses of the participants, with student and alumni/ae data in chapter three and faculty data in chapter four. The data is divided up into two chapters for two reasons: first, because a major piece of the study is comparative (student versus faculty ideals and perceptions), it seemed wise to keep the two data sets separate in order that each may speak fully on their own terms; and second, because each group of participants (students/alumni/ae and faculty) were asked to speak about both their ideals and their perceptions of IFL, the sheer volume of data collected necessitated separating out their responses into two chapters of more reasonable length. Data will be examined by dividing responses into "clusters of meaning," a term particular to phenomenological study that denotes groups of homogeneous information.

Once all of the clusters have been established, chapter five will then take a step back to look at the big picture of what was said and how it relates together. A more quantitative approach to the data will be taken in order to be able to see which clusters were most prevalent within the different study populations. It will also provide an opportunity to divide up the data in ways that will allow the reader to better determine which responses were connected to IFL ideals and which were related to IFL perceptions. From this vantage point, then, the *telos* of the hermeneutical phenomenological study will come to light: the "essence" statements, which will state *what* was experienced and *how* it was experienced by the participants.

Finally, chapter six will close out the study. It begins with a summary of the conclusions that could be drawn from the data, which then leads into some suggestions for the particular theatre department that participated in this venture. This is followed by some short reflections on the process of doing this research project, including thoughts on what was learned and what could have been done differently. Readers who desire more details may contact the author of the study.

With this groundwork laid, and the path ahead marked, attention must now turn to the literature that both supports this study and necessitates its existence. But one final, small note must be given before the page is turned. Throughout, the reader will find two different spellings of what many assume to be the same word: thea*ter* and thea*tre*. Both spellings are grammatically correct, and there is no formal rule governing the spelling of this word. However, in many American professional and educational circles there is an unstated and implicit understanding that *theater* refers to the physical space where a play or musical is performed, while *theatre* refers to the broader art form or to a production. *Theatre* is also the international spelling of the word, and hence has broader acceptance. For this paper this same distinction in spelling will be observed out of deference to the interdisciplinary and diverse audiences that this paper is directed toward.[6]

---

[6] This distinction was (thankfully) brought to my attention by Wesley Vander Lugt and Trevor Hart in their introduction to *Theatrical Theology: Explorations in Performing the Faith* (Eugene, OR: Cascade Books, 2014), xv.

# Literature Review

The literature that covers Christian faith and theatre is highly specialized. In many ways, it has to be: it naturally presupposes an interest by its audience in both matters of faith (and its practices) and in theatrical study. But even with such specialization the approaches and presuppositions on the part of authors vary. The majority write from the perspective of a pastor, worship arts leader, or other church member in order to explain how theatrical conventions can be appropriated for Church use.[1] Others, nearly always theologians, write from a theoretical framework, and wish to use theatrical language to explain God and/or God's relationship with the world at large.[2] And a very select few write as the voice of the theatre practitioner, by and for theatre artists, about faith in the craft.

This chapter seeks to lay a literary foundation for the study that follows. The challenge in creating such a foundation is that this study in particular draws upon a variety of related fields and subfields that connect to the intersection of Christianity and theatre. Or, to put it another way, the intersection of Christianity and theatre is not simply two roads meeting, but it is rather like a roundabout where several roads converge and flow together for a small period of time and space. Thus, though it does not have the depth found in an annotated bibliography, this chapter will provide the reader with at least a basic understanding of what literature merges into the roundabout traffic, and where that literature comes from.

In order to accurately reflect the breadth of material that has influenced this study, and in order to maintain a coherent structure for examining the literature, this chapter is divided into two categories: the first, loosely titled "Christian Faith," explores the relevant literature from practical theology and two of its sub-disciplines, religious education and spiritual formation, along with a few items of relevant literature related to faith integration within Christian college and university settings; the second category, "Theatrical Studies," pulls from sources within theatrical literature, specifically theatre education, spirituality within theatre, and finally the more narrow field of Christianity and theatre.

## Christian Faith

The field of practical theology is rich and diverse. It covers multiple areas of study, such as religious or Christian education, interreligious education, spiritual

---

[1] For example, see Jana Childers, *Performing the Word: Preaching as Theatre* (Nashville: Abingdon Press, 1998).

[2] Hans Urs von Balthasar, *Theo-Drama: Theological Dramatic Theory*, (5 vols. San Francisco: Ignatius Press, 1988), is perhaps the most influential and well-known example of this approach.

formation, spiritual care and counseling, preaching, evangelism, and pastoral care.[3] Bonnie Miller-McLemore defines it this way:

> Practical theology is a term commonly used in Christian theology for a general way of doing theology concerned with the embodiment of religious belief in the day-to-day lives of individuals and communities. Its subject matter is often described through generic words that suggest movement in time and space, such as action, practice, praxis, experience, situation, event, and performance. Its subject is also associated with action-oriented religious words, such as formation, transformation, discipleship, witness, ministry, and public mission.[4]

Because of its concern for embodied beliefs and located practices, practical theology is also the theological field most adept at interdisciplinary engagement. It generally has a greater preference for people rather than texts, and it is more and more being understood as a *method* for doing theology, which can be used to study just about anything.[5] It focuses on a "living human web" which seeks out connections between peoples, structures, and disciplines.[6]

Surprisingly, however, even with such a broad understanding of practical theology, within the academic field there has been nothing uncovered by the author that deals explicitly with practical theology and theatre as a practiced art form.[7]

---

[3] Richard Osmer, *Practical Theology: An Introduction* (Grand Rapids, MI: Eerdmans, 2008), 13.

[4] Bonnie Miller-McLemore, "Practical Theology," *Encyclopedia of Religion in America* (ed. Charles H. Lippy and Peter Williams; Thousand Oaks, CA: Congressional Quarterly Press, 2010), 1:1739–40.

[5] Kathleen Greider, class notes from "Seminar in Practical Theology" (lecture, Claremont School of Theology, Claremont, CA, September 14, 2011).

[6] Bonnie J. Miller-McLemore, "The Living Human Web: Pastoral Theology at the Turn of the Century," *Through the Eyes of Women* (ed. Jeanne Stevenson Moessner; Minneapolis: Augsburg Fortress, 1996), as cited in Osmer, *Practical Theology*, 16.

[7] It needs to be noted here that while the area of practical theology has largely ignored theatre, there has been a relative surge of literature within traditional theological studies that seeks to better formulate the way God interacts with God's creation. This is due in no small part to the groundbreaking opus of Hans Urs von Balthasar. Terms such as "theodrama," "theatrical theology," and "theological dramaturgy" have become important ways to describe the covenantal drama of humanity's relationship with God. In addition to von Balthasar, authors and texts to note in this area are Shannon Craigo-Snell, *The Empty Church: Theatre, Theology and Bodily Hope* (Oxford: Oxford University Press, 2014); Wesley Vander Lugt and Trevor Hart, eds., *Theatrical Theology*; also Wesley Vander Lugt, *Living Theodrama: Reimagining Theological Ethics* (Burlington, VT: Ashgate, 2014); Kevin Vanhoozer, *Faith Speaking Understanding: Performing the Drama of Doctrine* (Louisville: Westminster John Knox Press, 2014); and Ivan Khovacs, "Divine Reckonings in Profane Spaces: Towards a Theological Dramaturgy for Theatre" (PhD diss., University of Saint Andrews, 2007). And though, to the best of this author's knowledge, the connection has not been made in print, it is not that large of a leap to connect the work of certain evangelical practical theologians with theatre and/or theodrama. See in particular the concept of Christopraxis, first established in the work of Ray Anderson, *The Shape of Practical Theology* (Downers Grove, IL: Intervarsity Press, 2001) and expanded upon in his later works and in Andrew Root, *Christopraxis: A Practical Theology of the Cross* (Minneapolis: Fortress Press, 2014).

Though there has been the occasional foray into other narrative art forms,[8] theatre has been largely ignored. One can speculate that this is due to the long, contentious history between theatre and the church (particularly the Protestant churches), but a definitive answer can never be given. Whatever the reason, however, the scope of study must be broadened to include authors who might not self-identify as practical theologians but who, by the very nature of their work, fall within its broad and porous borders. The first such group would be those who engage in religious education.

*Religious Education*

Within the field of religious education, or Christian education, as it is commonly referred to within Protestant evangelical circles, educators have been drawing on theatrical conventions for the better part of 100 years, though the Roman Catholic Church might rightly scoff at such a short time span and point out that known theatrical pedagogies were employed as early as the seventh century AD.[9] As puritanical influences began to wane within the American church scene,[10] many Christians saw the theatre as a powerful tool for sharing the gospel and teaching its precepts. Religious educators began writing texts about incorporating storytelling into their instruction, or using dramatic performance as a pedagogical tool. The purpose for such integration ranged from moral instruction to biblical exegesis.[11] These books and articles were nearly always written by and for the Church; though there was often attention given to theatrical techniques and conventions (e.g., lighting, costuming, direction), there was never any real engagement with theatre professionals. The centuries of mistrust between the two groups saw to that. Religious educators and pastors largely understood the theatrical craft to be a supplement to traditional sermons, exegesis, and more traditional techniques. Thus, in most books of religious education from the twentieth century one finds theatre as a tool for the sanctuary or Sunday-school classroom in order to make learning more engaging. This "theatre as a tool" approach is utilized by most practitioners and

---

[8] See, for example, Jörg Herrmann, "'Collide with Destiny!' Religion in the Popular Cinema of the Nineties," *International Journal of Practical Theology* 6.1 (2002): 49–63.

[9] Herbert Sennett, *Religion and Dramatics: The Relationship between Christianity and the Theater Arts* (Lanham, MD: University Press of America, 1995), tells of Amalarius, the Bishop of Metz (c. 780–850), who presented an allegorical interpretation of the Mass as a theatrical trope.

[10] For an excellent treatment on the history of the American Protestant churches and their relationship to the theatre, please see Claudia Durst Johnson, *Church and Stage: The Theatre as Target of Religious Condemnation in 19th Century America* (Jefferson, NC: McFarland & Co., 2008).

[11] Respectively, Edward Porter St. John, Stories and Story-Telling in Moral and Religious Education (Boston: Pilgrim Press, 1910); and David Torbett, "'I Did Not Wash My Feet with that Woman': Using Dramatic Performance to Teach Biblical Studies," *Teaching Theology and Religion* 13.4 (2010): 307–19.

authors, including Christelle Estrada, Patricia Griggs, Susan Shaw, David Torbett, and Carleton Wood, among others.[12]

A secondary subset of religious educators uses certain theatrical conventions, such as storytelling, as a means of communicating religious truths with their students or congregants. These authors generally are not interested in actually performing theatre or taking in professional productions, but rather are using elements that are native to these fields in order to promote creative thinking about a biblical story, moral dilemma, or ethical imperative, or to foster a sense of community and/or cultural understanding. This is most evident in the writings of Frank Rogers, Jr., Jana Childers, Sue Phillips, Charles Boyd, Jeanette Perkins Brown, and Peter Pitzele, among others.[13] Finally, still other religious educators prefer to take a historical approach to theatre study as a means of understanding how the church and the narrative arts have arrived at their current relationship. Claudia Durst Johnson, though not a formal religious educator, has thoroughly shown through her own scholarship that the church and the theatre have a long way to go in order to heal the fractured and difficult relationship that has existed for centuries. Her book *Church and Stage* provides vital context for any religious education scholar looking to utilize theatre within their own work.[14]

Even though the majority of Christian educators use theatre as a pedagogical tool, a method for interpretation or appropriation, or a lens through which to view history, in more recent years a few Christian educators have written either as active theatre practitioners or have co-authored works with theatre artists in order to get their professional perspective. John Steven Paul, former chair of the Theater Department at Valparaiso University (d. 2009), wrote about his department and the way they sought to integrate faith into their instruction, his leadership, and the opportunities given to students.[15] Herbert Sennett, in his book *Religion and*

---

[12] Christelle L. Estrada, *Telling Stories Like Jesus Did: Creative Parables for Teachers* (San Jose: Resource Publications, 1987); Patricia Griggs, *Using Storytelling in Christian Education* (Nashville: Abingdon Press, 1981); Susan M. Shaw, *Storytelling in Religious* Education (Birmingham, AL: Religious Education Press, 1999); Torbett, "'I Did Not Wash My Feet'"; Carleton W. Wood, *The Dramatic Method in Religious Education* (New York: Abingdon Press, 1931). See also Margaret W. Eggleston, *Use of the Story in Religious Education* (New York: Harper & Brothers Publishers, 1936).

[13] Frank Rogers, *Finding God in the Graffiti: Empowering Teenagers Through Stories* (Cleveland: Pilgrim Press, 2011); Childers, *Performing the Word;* Sue Phillips, "Reflection on Classroom Practice: the Theater of Learning," *International Journal of Children's Spirituality* 8.1 (2003): 55–66; Charles Arthur Boyd, *Worship in Drama: A Manual of Methods and Materials for Young People and their Leaders* (Philadelphia: Judson Press, 1924); Jeanette Perkins Brown, *The Storyteller in Religious Education* (Boston: Pilgrim Press, 1951); Peter Pitzele, *Scripture Windows: Towards a Practice of Bibliodrama* (Los Angeles: Torah Aura Productions, 1998). See also Yolanda Smith, "The Table: Christian Education as Performative Art," *Religious Education* 103.3 (2008): 301–05.

[14] Johnson, *Church and Stage.*

[15] John Steven Paul, "'I Love To Tell the Story': *Teaching Theater at a Church-Related College,"* *Teaching as an Act of Faith: Theory and Practice in Church-Related Higher Education* (ed. Arlin C. Migliazzo; New York: Fordham University Press, 2002), 163–87.

*Dramatics*, examines how the church can support theatre arts, which at least shows an awareness of the value of engaging professional artists in the life of the church (though it does not appear that he actively sought out professional input in his book).[16] And in what is undoubtedly the best book on the subject, theologian Todd Johnson teams up with professional theatre artist and educator Dale Savidge to examine the relationship between theatre and theology, of which more will be said later.[17] These few authors aside, however, theatre seems to be largely absent from the lexicon of religious education.

*Spiritual Formation*

The second area of practical theology that draws attention because of its connection with this study is spiritual formation. Spiritual formation, popularly defined as the "intentional Christian practice that has as its goal the development of spiritual maturity that leads to Christ-likeness,"[18] is concerned with how Christians live because of the transforming work of God in their lives. In a more careful definition, Jeffrey P. Greenman, President at Regent College and editor of the book *Life in the Spirit*, writes, "Spiritual formation is our continuing response to the reality of God's grace shaping us into the likeness of Jesus Christ, through the work of the Holy Spirit, in the community of faith, for the sake of the world."[19] Within evangelical expression, this definition highlights the core tenets of how Christians should approach their faith: first, it has a strong Biblical foundation, where the reality of God's grace is found manifest; second, it is cross-focused, not self-centered, as evident by the central focus on Jesus Christ, whom Christians are to emulate; third, it alludes to the process of conversion or being "born again," which requires the salvific presence of the Holy Spirit in the life and work of the believer; and finally, it shows an outward focus on active participation in doing good in the world and in the communities of faith where the believer is located for the greater glory of God. These four tenets—also referred to as Biblicism, Crucicentrism, Conversionism, and Activism—are understood to be important parts of how the Christian approaches and engages in spiritual formation.[20]

Spiritual formation literature within evangelical Christianity is relatively new. Because of their initial emphatic and intentional departure from anything appearing to be connected to the Roman Catholic Church, and because of their

---

[16] Sennett, *Religion and Dramatics*.

[17] Todd E. Johnson and Dale Savidge, *Performing the Sacred: Theology and Theatre in Dialogue* (Grand Rapids: Baker Academic, 2009).

[18] "Spiritual Formation," Wikipedia, last modified August 1, 2015 https://web.archive.org/web/20150819212310.

[19] Jeffrey P. Greenman and George Kalantzis, "Spiritual Formation in Theological Perspective," *Life in the Spirit: Spiritual Formation in Theological Perspective* (ed. Jeffrey P. Greenman and George Kalantzis; Downers Grove, IL: IVP Academic, 2010), 24.

[20] Greenman and Kalantzis, "Spiritual Formation," 23–35.

Puritanical roots, the evangelically oriented churches in the United States shunned many of the ascetic and/or mystical influences from the medieval era, influences which brought with them an emphasis on spiritual formation through practices such as solitude, fasting, and meditation. Thus, while many mainline Protestant denominations began to explore avenues of spiritual formation during the nineteenth and twentieth centuries, many fundamentalist and evangelical congregations and denominations felt it was a backdoor for demonic influences to undermine the work of the church.[21] Richard Foster's seminal book *Celebration of Discipline*, though still regarded as suspect in some fundamentalist circles, can be understood as the unofficial rediscovery of spiritual disciplines and formation by evangelicals.[22] And though his work has been widely influential in evangelical circles, it is largely because of the writings of Dallas Willard (d. 2013), former Professor of Philosophy at the University of Southern California, that spiritual formation as an evangelical academic discipline really took root. Willard was a founding member of the *Journal of Spiritual Formation and Soul Care*, a respected scholar on Edmund Husserl, and the author of a dozen different books, the majority of which dealt with the topic of spiritual formation. With his intellectual acumen and his ability to write in a manner that could attract both laymen and scholars alike, Willard revitalized an area of Christian faith within evangelicalism that had long lay dormant. His five central texts on holiness and spiritual formation are still in wide circulation and use after his death.[23]

Because spiritual formation within evangelical literature is relatively new, it is still developing and finding its application into other areas of life. Consequently, there is virtually nothing written about its relation to the theatrical arts. There are some authors outside of evangelicalism who have begun to explore the relationship between theatre and spiritual formation however. Fredericka Berger, through the Center for the Arts and Religion at Wesley Theological Seminary, wrote a paper

---

[21] This attitude still can be found today. A simple Google search for "Richard Foster AND New Age" yields multiple websites that seek to call to the church away from "'Christian' mysticism—currently crippling the evangelical community through the spurious Spiritual Forma-tion as taught by Foster along with his spiritual twin Dallas Willard." Quote from Ken Silva, "The Cult of Guru Richard Foster," *Apprising Ministries:* https://web.archive.org/web/20150522031810 (accessed September 27, 2015).

[22] Richard J. Foster, *Celebration of Discipline: The Path to Spiritual Growth* (San Francisco: Harper & Row, 1978).

[23] Dallas Willard, *In Search of Guidance: Developing a Conversational Relationship with God* (Ventura, CA: Regal Books, 1984); *The Spirit of the Disciplines: Understanding How God Changes Lives* (San Francisco: Harper and Row, 1988); *The Divine Conspiracy: Rediscovering Our Hidden Life in God* (San Francisco: Harper One, 1997); *Renovation of the Heart: Putting on the Character of Christ* (Colorado Springs: NavPress, 2002); *Knowing Christ Today: Why We Can Trust Spiritual Knowledge* (San Francisco: HarperCollins Press, 2009). *In Search of Guidance* has since been revised and republished under the name *Hearing God: Developing a Conversational Relationship with God* (Downers Grove, IL: Intervarsity Press, 1999). Willard died in 2013 from cancer.

that explored the way spiritual formation could occur through drama.[24] Through it tended to default toward theatrical pedagogy within religious education, it nonetheless warrants a mention here because it makes the connection between theatrical practices and formation. *Body and Bible*, edited by Björn Krondorfer, is a book on Bibliodrama—a role-playing form of exegetical expression that uses theatricality to explore the meanings within biblical texts[25]—that makes occasional connections to the way that enacting biblical narratives assists in "meaning-making" and the spiritual formation of the participants.[26] However, like Berger's work, it tends to play on the outskirts of spiritual formation as a field of study without seeking or exploring a direct link between the two fields. In a similar vein, though with different intentions, theologians like Kevin Vanhoozer have written books that deal with the "drama" or "theatre" of God, usually from a more traditional theological vantage point. Occasionally these works veer into the realm of spiritual formation. In his book *Faith Speaking Understanding*,[27] Vanhoozer writes about the need for Christ followers to be actively engaged in "learning the part" of becoming "Little Christs." Though his engagement is mostly contained to pastoral exhortations to live out the faith, his choice to use theatrical imagery and language shows his awareness of how theatre can and does influence the spiritual formation of those who partake of its richness. There are others, many of whom are mentioned in above notes, who use theatricality in the way Vanhoozer does, but sadly they too seem to miss what could be a rich and invigorating field of study, the interplay between theatrical engagement and its role in the spiritual formation of viewers and practitioners.

The material that seems to take the process of spiritual formation most seriously in relation to theatrical practice is from Frank Rogers' *Finding God in the Graffiti*. While the book is dedicated to discussing narrative pedagogy and how it can be used with teens, chapter three in particular is devoted to discussing how story crafting can "mediate a profound experience of the sacred."[28] The chapter uses the term "contemplative encounters" and provides examples and suggestions on how to use narrative to foster such encounters, but the overall essence of the chapter revolves around using storytelling and story creation to foster a space for spiritual formation to take place. Though this formation is largely disassociated with approaches that "nurture a mere cognitive familiarity with a story or a deepened

---

[24] Fredericka Berger, "Spiritual Formation Through Drama," *ARTS Journal* 15.1 (2003): 34–45.

[25] Jeffrey Tirrell, "Bibliodrama," *Encyclopedia of Christian Education* (ed. George Thomas Kurian and Mark A. Lamport; Lanham, MD: Rowman and Littlefield, 2015), 1:147–48. For a more complete description of Bibliodrama see the authoritative work by Peter Pitzele, *Scripture Windows*.

[26] Björn Krondorfer, ed., *Body and Bible: Interpreting and Experiencing Biblical Narratives* (Philadelphia: Trinity Press International, 1992).

[27] Vanhoozer, *Faith Speaking Understanding*.

[28] Frank Rogers, "How Do Stories Mediate a Profound Experience of the Sacred?" *Finding God in the Graffiti*, 74–97.

intellectual understanding of that story's context and meaning," it can help many people "feel the soulful realities from which the sacred stories were first written" and "encounter the sacred presence with which these narratives are saturated."[29] While the point of the book is not formation per se it is one of the few that take seriously the formative role of theatrical experiences and names it as such.

*Faith Integration in Christian Colleges and Universities*

While both Religious/Christian ducation and spiritual formation are relevant fields within practical theology, some attention must also be paid to literature that is particular to the interdisciplinary nature of this study. Specifically, is there any literature that seeks to do what this study does, or that is similar enough in nature that it can provide data relevant to the research done here?

There are three texts that deal specifically with the integration of faith and learning within Christian college or university settings and are appropriate for our context. The first is a case study of how an undergraduate Biblical studies professor used an assignment which required students to research and dramatically perform a biblical story as part of the exegetical learning process. David Torbett, a professor at Marietta College, wrote a brief synopsis of his use of theatrical learning in his Biblical studies class, where he sought to combine traditional methods of learning, such as commentary research, with more engaged and active learning found in theatrical studies.[30] He did this in part because "biblical literature in particular has an intrinsic dramatic quality that is especially compatible with dramatic performance," making it "an effective teaching tool in biblical studies courses."[31] His article articulates both the value of theatrical learning and how it can be used in other contexts, such as a biblical studies course. This is relevant because it illustrates how theatrical learning can be a catalyst for religious learning, and how religious material and study can provide the impetus and context for theatrical engagement.

> These students had taken a step towards learning for themselves what many biblical studies professors have struggled to explain: that there is no uninterpreted text, and that the meaning of the text is always shaped—to an extent—by the mind (and the dramatic imagination) of the reader."[32]

Thus there is evidence that other people, in other fields, have discovered that theatre and faith coexist in ways that enhance student learning and awareness about beliefs and formation.

The second text is entitled, "'I Love to Tell the Story': Teaching Theater at a Church-Related College," by John Steven Paul, in the book *Teaching as an Act of Faith: Theory and Practice in Church-Related Higher Education.*[33] In the chapter

---

[29] Rogers, "How Do Stories Mediate a Profound Experience of the Sacred?" 81–82.

[30] Torbett, "'I Did Not Wash My Feet,'" 307–19.

[31] Torbett, "'I Did Not Wash My Feet,'" 310.

[32] Torbett, "'I Did Not Wash My Feet,'" 311.

[33] Paul, "'I Love To Tell the Story,'" 63–187.

16

Paul provides practical theatre pedagogy, course suggestions, and a list of the five fundamental principles to which his particular theatre department subscribes:

1) Theater pedagogy is most effectively delivered in the form of doing rather than talking;
2) The actor-audience dynamic is the essence of theater art;
3) Theater is a community of artists and craftspersons formed around a project and committed to a goal. A play is projected into a community and will affect that community;
4) Art is the fruit of our labors and to God we owe the first fruits;
5) Theater is a vocation; it is a calling that can be lived in any number of careers.

Many of these principles coincide with information found in *Performing the Sacred*, and they provide an example of what faith integration may look like in a department that is endeavoring to live it out in practical and educationally-based ways.

Paul also addresses theatrical concerns from a distinctly educational *and* theological perspective. For instance, Paul writes about the dichotomy of the actor's motivation. An actor is always intrinsically selfish, he says, while at the same time generous. An actor always wants to be in the limelight, but at the same time the nature of the craft demands that she give her performance to the audience with no regard for how they will accept it. In a Christian setting this generosity should be highlighted and expanded to include attitudes toward fellow actors and playwrights. This can foster a sense of community and camaraderie which is not only in line with the command of Christ to "love thy neighbor," but which is also an effective part of the integration of faith and learning, as evidenced by the data collected for this research project and which will be shared shortly.

Finally, Paul also writes about the different intentional ministries of his department. He has teams of students who do free performances at public schools to talk about sexual abuse issues. He also has teams that write and create performance homilies which can be inserted into Sunday sermons at churches. Both teams have different foci, but both require generosity of time and energy on the part of the students. The second team in particular was created as a way of giving back "firstfruits" to God, and Paul calls this type of team "drama ministry" in a very intentional way. This type of "practiced" integration of faith and theatrical enterprise with an intentional heart toward *service* also appeared in the data collected for this study as an important part of student idealized and perceived faith integration. Thus in all respects, from theatrical theory to theological ideals to practical application, this chapter provides supporting evidence for the data collected and examples of how that information might be applied.

The last text that deals with the integration of faith and learning within Christian college or university settings is an article that is the foundational source upon which this study is based. In a qualitative research study of one hundred and twenty undergraduate students from seven different schools within the Council for Christian Colleges and Universities, authors Michael Sherr, George Huff, and Mary

Curran set out to discover student perceptions of IFL.[34] They themselves believed that there is a "negligible amount of empirical studies on the subject" of IFL,[35] specifically dealing with student perceptions, and sought to fill the gap in the literature. In their research they discovered that two main categories influenced student perceptions of IFL: "faculty relationships," specifically their relationships with God and with the students; and "faculty competence" with respect to faith integration within the curriculum and in creating a classroom environment which fostered "belonging, acceptance, and commitment."[36] Faculty who were able to create the most effective IFL experiences were those who did it in natural and unforced ways. This research proved to be exceptionally helpful in forming the current study, but it also had one glaring limitation, namely that it did not differentiate between majors. Would theatre students respond in the same way that business majors would? Or psychology? Or nursing? It was therefore determined that undertaking a follow-up study could be beneficial for furthering the research done by Sherr, Huff, and Curran to show whether it may have broad application; and it could also provide a resource for intentional IFL within the performing arts.

**Theatrical Studies**

With the quick foray through the literature of the disciplines of practical theology and college faith integration finished, attention must now be given to relevant literature written from the side of theatrical studies. If practical theology and traditional IFL literature do not have much to say on the subject of faith integration among collegiate theatre artists, is there anything that has been written in theatre studies that might enhance or support what this study aims to do? As in the first half of this chapter, in order to best answer this question the next section will be separated into three subdivisions. First will be a brief examination of any relevant theatre education literature. Since this study took place in an educational setting, might this area provide any new perspectives or insights? Next will be a look into the literature that seeks to explicitly examine the role or place of spirituality within theatre studies. Though faith integration and spirituality are distinct subspecialties there may be crossover literature that is germane to our purposes. And finally, the chapter will conclude with a scan of any applicable literature that relates specifically to the intersection of Christianity and theatre.

*Theatre Education*

As a subspecialty within theatrical studies, theatre education usually refers to the training of students to teach theatre in K–12 settings. It broadly seeks to equip future educators with the tools to use theatrical learning within the classroom, after-

---

[34] Michael Sherr, George Huff, and Mary Curran, "Student Perceptions of Salient Indicators of Integration of Faith and Learning (IFL): The Christian Vocation Model," *Journal of Research on Christian Education* 16.1 (2007): 15–33.

[35] Sherr, Huff, and Curran, "Student Perceptions," 17.

[36] Sherr, Huff, and Curran, "Student Perceptions," 24.

school programs, or in certain types of social activism. Generally speaking, this means that theatre education students learn the basics of theatre: directing, casting, staging, terminology, producing, etc., and how it can be used in nontraditional settings. On occasion there is discussion about acting techniques, such as those of Stanislavski or Meisner, but generally it is focused on how to properly use and communicate theatrical information in order to be an effective teacher. Because of its educational bent, and because of the embodied approach to learning that theatrical practice can offer, it might be expected that certain texts could include faith-based content to engage the practitioner's spirituality. After all, if theatrical learning is geared toward engaging the body, emotions, and mind of the individual or group, why not the soul?

However, whether out of ignorance, attempts to be inclusive, willful blindness, or some other undisclosed reason, the primary authors who write within this field seem to ignore faith integration and instead focus on pedagogy, history, or the challenges of working in two fields (theatre and teaching). Tony Jackson's great work, *Learning Through Theatre*, centers around examining the way the "Theatre In Education" movement from Great Britain has influenced learning;[37] Barbara McKean's *A Teaching Artist at Work* focuses on the growing field of teaching artistry and the challenges that come with working both as a professional artist and as a teacher;[38] Philip Taylor's *Applied Theatre* focuses on using theatre as an engaged, pedagogical approach to raise social awareness of located issues in a community;[39] and multiple other texts focus on teaching theatre to particular populations or age groups.[40] Unfortunately, none of the texts mentioned here address the role of faith in theatre practice.

There are *very* few authors who talk about religion in relation to theatre education, and those who do generally approach it from the ambiguous and generic term "spirituality." Joan Lazarus, in her book *Signs of Change: New Directions in Theater Education*, has a brief section on spirituality within theatre, and Joe Winston published an article in the *International Journal of Children's Spirituality* in 2002 that looked at theatre education in the United Kingdom from a spiritual

---

[37] Tony Jackson, *Learning Through Theatre: New Perspectives on Theatre in Education* (2nd ed.; New York: Routledge, 1993).

[38] Barbara McKean, *A Teaching Artist at Work: Theatre with Young People in Educational Settings* (Portsmouth, NH: Heinemann, 2006).

[39] Philip Taylor, *Applied Theatre: Creating Transformative Encounters in the Community* (Portsmouth, NH: Heinemann, 2003).

[40] Examples abound. See, for example, Ian McCurrach and Barbara Darnley, *Special Talents, Special Needs: Drama for People with Learning Disabilities* (Philadelphia: Jessica Kingsley Publishers, 1999); or Gail Skroback Hennessey, *Reader's Theater Scripts: Improve Fluency, Vocabulary and Comprehension: Grades 6–8* (Huntington Beach, CA: Shell Education, 2010).

perspective.[41] But these are not the normative approaches to the field. A search of journal publications that cover theatre education yielded no results when terms like "faith" or "Christian" were entered.[42] It thus appears to be up to the individual practitioner, instructor, or teaching artist to determine what, if any, faith-based approach should be included in their instruction, and how best to do it. And so, unfortunately, the field of theatre education has little to say with regard to faith integration, particularly from the Christian tradition.

*Spirituality in Theatre*

So if there is little of note in the theatre education literature relating to faith integration, or seemingly to spiritual matters at all, does that mean theatre does not acknowledge the spiritual dimension of humanity? Of course not. In fact, even though theatre education authors rarely write about matters of faith, the broader theatre literature is quite open to acknowledging the power of spirituality within theatre practice.[43] The most notable of these must be Peter Brook's *The Empty Space*.[44] Brook, the former Director of Productions for the Royal Shakespeare Company and a winner of the Tony Award, Emmy Award, Lawrence Olivier Award, and numerous other distinguished prizes, is also a prolific author who has penned eight different books about theatre. His first book, *The Empty Space*, provides perhaps the clearest window into how many theatre practitioners understand spirituality and faith in their craft. Though he does not set out to discuss spirituality in theatre, one of the world's foremost directors is keenly aware of the role spirituality plays in the way theatre interacts with its patrons and participants. In his identification of four different "meanings" of "theatre," Brook sets forth that theatre is Deadly, Holy, Rough, and Immediate. Though all of these intersect with spirituality in some fashion, Holy theatre is the one most profound in its connection. As he states in the opening of his chapter on Holy theatre, "I am calling it the Holy Theatre for short, but it could be called The Theatre of the Invisible-Made-Visible:

---

[41] Joan Lazarus, Signs of Change: *New Directions in Theater Education* (Chicago: University of Chicago Press, 2012); Joe Winston, "Drama, Spirituality and the Curriculum," *International Journal of Children's Spirituality* 7.3 (2002): 241–55.

[42] These include the *Journal of Applied Theatre and Performance, the Educational Theatre Journal*, the *Applied Theatre Researcher,* and the *Teaching Artist Journal,* as well as searches in broader, web-based academic search databases (e.g., Ebscohost, ProQuest and Academic Search Premier).

[43] Examples include Daniel Meyer-Dinkgräfe, *Observing Theatre: Spirituality and Subjectivity in the Performing Arts* (New York: Rodopi, 2013); Rebecca Ann Rugg, "Dramaturgy as Devotion: 365 Days/365 Plays of Suzan-Lori Parks," *PAJ: A Journal of Performance and Art* 31.91 (2009): 68–79; Edmund B. Lingan's wonderful overview of spirituality in the arts in "The Alchemical Marriage of Art, Performance and Spirituality," *PAJ: A Journal of Performance and Art* 31.1 (2009): 38–43; and Benjamin Lloyd, "Stanislavsky, Spirituality and the Problem of the Wounded Actor," *New Theater Quarterly* 22.85 (2006): 70–75.

[44] Peter Brook, *The Empty Space* (1968; repr., New York: Viking Penguin, Inc., 1988).

the notion that the stage is a place where the invisible can appear has a deep hold on our thoughts."[45] He continues,

> The theatre is the last forum where idealism is still an open question: many audiences all over the world will answer positively from their own experience that they have seen the face of the invisible through an experience on the stage that transcended their experience in life…. More than ever, we crave for an experience that is beyond the humdrum. Some look for it in jazz, classical music, in marijuana and in LSD. In the theatre we shy away from the holy because we don't know what this could be— we only know what is called the holy has let us down…. A holy theatre not only presents the invisible but also offers conditions that make its perception possible.[46]

From this it becomes clear that what he is describing is what theologians struggle to communicate in sermons and books: the creation of incarnational space where the "Invisible-Made-Visible" dwells. From an evangelical, theological standpoint we might use the word "God" or "the Holy Spirit" to speak of the One we encounter; Brook, as a theatre artist who does not speak about his faith (or lack thereof), still acknowledges that through his craft space can be made where the Holy can be encountered. It is, in perhaps a more pagan sense, a church: it seeks to create a space where people gather to see "the face of the invisible." He interestingly (and rightly) states that many people, both in the theatre and outside of it, have been "let down" by the "holy," meaning that they have sought after it but have only found ephemeral and unfulfilling promises of lasting connections that transcend the drudgery of daily life. But theatre, by its embodied, incarnate, and communal nature provides a space where we can rightly perceive that which is beyond ourselves. This perception, and the encounter that can arise from it, is Brook's understanding of theatrical spirituality.

If this kind of spirituality seems a far cry from traditional Christian theology, it is. But it is by no means unique to Brook. Robert Wuthnow, a Professor of Sociology at Princeton, wrote a book entitled *Creative Spirituality*, which largely consists of interviews with artists of all different ilks, including theatre artists.[47] In the book is found this same understanding of art as a means of "making visible" that which otherwise might be lost in the frenetic pace of daily life. Though some artists in the book held to a more Christian perspective of faith and spirituality (e.g., Madeleine L'Engle), most would have felt very comfortable with Brook's description. This is supported by similar research done by Roger Grainger, a professor in South Africa who asked actors to describe what "acting [is] really

---

[45] Brook, *Empty Space*, 47.

[46] Brook, *Empty Space*, 47–48, 53–54, 63.

[47] Robert Wuthnow, *Creative Spirituality: The Way of the Artist* (Berkeley: University of California Press, 2001).

about."[48] Their responses provide "evidence for the claim that theatre is itself an inherently spiritual medium (as well as a vehicle for explicitly religious plays), and that the relationship of professional actors to their craft may be considered to be implicitly religious."[49] This spirituality is often expressed in oblique ways, but it usually refers to experiences similar to what Brook describes, and that serve to unite the actors with each other and/ or with the audience in ways that transcend language or space. As one actor in Grainger's article explains,

> there are moments when all these differences seem to vanish and you become one; one with the author, one with your fellow actors and one with your audience. The soul, the essence of ourselves is the only thing we have in common. I believe it is the only thing that everyone can experience at the same moment. In order for them to experience it, I have to get out of the way. The actor must transmit from the stage the great gestures of the human soul and show them, and not himself, to the spectator.[49]

This unity is how most theatrical literature describes and understands spirituality. But in an obviously Christian setting like a faith-based university theatre program, this type of response would likely be only half of the answer. So are there theatre artists and authors who are writing from a distinctly Christian vantage point?

*Christianity in Theatre*

Though they are few, there are some authors who are writing about the intersection of Christian faith integration and theatre. Todd Johnson (a theologian) and Dale Savidge (a theatre artist) have co-written a book called *Performing the Sacred*, which seeks to examine the points of commonality between theatre and theology. It is the most comprehensive and wellstructured book on the market today. It seeks to understand the historical relationship between the artistic medium and the Church, and then posits points of commonality between the disciplines that can serve as hooks for future conversation. Johnson and Savidge write from the perspective of Christians who are both artists and theologians, not as people engaging in one field and trying to appropriate the other. It is designed for artists who strive to work in all settings, including professionally, and it is not catering solely to the "church drama" crowd like so many other texts. It takes the ethical dilemmas faced by actors and playwrights in contemporary theatre seriously, but unlike many of their contemporaries, they move beyond ethical questions to examine the broad theology of the theatrical process, explaining it as a human and divine enterprise (Incarnation), a corporate enterprise (Community), and a transformative encounter (Presence). They frame their intention in the following way:

---

[48] Roger Grainger, "The Faith of Actors: *Implicit Religion* and Acting," *Implicit Religion* 8.2 (2005): 166–177. 49 Grainger, "Faith of Actors," 166.

[49] Grainger, "Faith of Actors," 170.

The approach taken... is not to ask just what theatre has to do with theology, but also to ask what theology has to do with theatre. In other words, what does theatre mean theologically, and how does it do so? What theological categories can be used to evaluate the theatrical event, and how might we appreciate the art and craft of theatre, relative to the other arts, from the perspective of Christian theology? How does theatre as an art form uniquely reflect the *imago Dei*?[50]

Thus, these theological concepts (Incarnation, Community and Presence) are present within any type of theatrical process or production and are broad enough for general application. Interestingly, they also write from the perspective of a theatrical audience, illustrating how people can engage with a theatrical piece in the same way that they might engage and critique films from a theological perspective. This text is particularly important because it provides both a theological framework and a theatrical knowledge, which support some of the data in this research: as will be shown, themes like *community* and *presence* appear in the interviews and observations that arose from them.

Besides Johnson and Savidge, there is a small number of other authors who also examine the intersection of Christianity and theatre from an artistic perspective, though usually not as directly or intentionally. These include Madeleine L'Engle, who, though her focus is primarily on creativity and art in the broader sense, still writes of theatre reverently as an art form where truth is revealed and which has an "element of transcendence";[51] Shannon Craigo-Snell, whose study of performance interpretation and the comparison of theatrical play-making with Christian interpretation of Scripture is powerfully presented;[52] Kay Baxter, whose dated yet helpful text presents an examination of various plays and their theological significance, along with the significance they play in society at large;[53] and John Steven Paul, whose article was referenced earlier in this chapter.

Thus, though it is clear that good material exists, there are yet still gaping holes in the study of the intersection of Christianity and theatre arts, which is why this study is being done. And so, with this cursory examination of the general fields

---

[50] Johnson and Savidge, *Performing the Sacred*, 56–57.

[51] Madeleine L'Engle, *Walking on Water: Reflections on Faith and Art* (1980; repr., New York: North Point Press, 1995), 73, 146. This is likely due to the fact that her husband is an actor.

[52] Shannon Craigo-Snell, "Command Performance: Rethinking Performance Interpretation in the Context of Divine Discourse," *Modern Theology* 16.4 (2000): 475–94. Though she is not a professional theatre educator/artist, her discussion of theatre clearly shows an awareness of how the craft is practiced, used, and understood by theatre artists.

[53] Though it was also written more from a theological perspective than that of a theatre artist, the general tenor and tone of Baxter's book are more in line with Peter Brook than von Balthasar. Take, for example, the following quote: "Is drama possible without mystery? What does it mean when order, 'degree' is shattered? This question inflames the imagination of a great playwright, because it brings to full consciousness our ignorance about Being, our unpredictability, or irrationality and, for Christians, our need for God's grace." Kay M. Baxter, *Contemporary Theatre and the Christian Faith* (New York: Abingdon Press, 1964), 49 (emphasis original).

that this book will traverse complete, let us now turn our attention to the study at hand.

# Description of the Study

## What Is Being Studied?

This study seeks to answer the question of how faculty and students in an undergraduate Christian theatre department understand faith integration in their field. It approaches the question in two different ways: first, how do both groups (faculty and students) envision faith integration happening in an ideal situation or setting? Second, how do both groups perceive faith integration, and any subsequent spiritual formation, happening within their department? The intention is that through the interview process both students and faculty would share their dreams and ideas of effective faith integration, as well as their own experiences with it in their classrooms, productions, and encounters. This information would thus examine the current state of affairs within the department, as well as the imagined or future-oriented desires of those who have devoted their academic careers to the craft.

It is hypothesized that while most Christian university or college theatre departments have a desire to integrate faith and spiritual formation into their programs, many of them are not doing it as effectively as they imagine. It is also hypothesized that most Christian theatre department faculty are unaware of the way spiritual formation is happening within their departments, and that this lack of awareness is leading to false assumptions or missed opportunities for faith integration to occur. Finally, based on previous faith integration studies done with general student populations, it is hypothesized that the role of faculty and staff as mentors and models of faith integration is the top factor in theatre students' spiritual formation, more so than coursework, assignments, or self-study during productions.

## Rationale for the Study

This study developed out of the author's own perceptions of faith integration and experiences of working in theatre, both in educational and professional settings. The concept initially evolved from experiences as a student studying theatre at a Christian university, where there seemed to be very little interaction between faith and theatrical studies. The two fields seemed distant and unrelated; it was intellectually known that God was in the arts and that the arts were a way of glorifying God, but that knowledge did not translate into visible action. If this disconnect was present in a Christian theatre department at an evangelical Christian university, it appeared even more clearly afterwards, once the author was exposed to the broader sphere of public theatre. This author thus began to wonder who else might have experienced this type of secular/sacred division, and developed the desire to study the narrative arts and theology in tandem. It has since manifested as a clearer desire to study how faith integration is occurring (or even *if* it is occurring) in the current curriculums and created experiences of student Christian artists today.

Because of this history, this study has personal significance for many reasons. First, any artist who has been involved in live theatre for a length of time (the author has been involved in live theatre for the better part of twenty years) has seen the powerful impact it can have on people. Both anecdotal experiences and scientific studies have shown that people are far more likely to change their attitude or behavior toward something (or someone) if emotional persuasion is involved; simply trying to logically or empirically prove or disprove the point rarely produces the same affective change.[1] When the author began to delve into the world of biblical academics it was quickly discovered that much of the material used was rather dry and lifeless; though it was well reasoned, it rarely had any lasting impact in the way that a powerfully told film or theatrical piece could. In short, there appeared to be something about the human condition which associates emotional response with mental assent or dissent. Thus, it seemed only logical that there were things that artists could teach theologians. Conversely, theologians could also teach artists about the wisdom, insights, and nuances that are required to tell the Christian story (or even a Christian virtue) faithfully. Many artists tend to sacrifice detail for the larger story, a somewhat lazy approach that can be dangerous when dealing with religious or theological material (hence the evangelical response to Darren Aronofsky's *Noah*).[2] Thus, the training of artists to think about philosophical assumptions, worldviews, and historical understandings about God, Jesus, heaven, etc., can be exceedingly helpful in creating work that is faithful to what the artist or artistic community actually believes. These two fields must engage in mutually constructive dialogue.

A second reason this study is personally significant is because of the author's own experience of disconnect between faith and artistic endeavors while an undergraduate theatre student at a Christian university. The atmosphere of the theater created a false dichotomy between the *sacred*, i.e., chapel services, bible classes, church, etc.; and the *secular*, i.e., theatre classes and productions. While this dichotomy was not necessarily real, nor was it likely intentionally created by

---

[1] Psychology has also shown that connections exist between emotion and decision making. One particular area of research, known as dual process theory, postulates that human beings have two systems, one that is emotion-based and the other that is rationale-based, which compete in a person's moral reasoning processes. Thus, for example, a person who was raised to believe that homosexuality is immoral might be more inclined to change her mind and accept it as moral if she had a strong emotional desire (such as having gay friends and desiring to see them be happy) that could override the learned, cognitive position she previously held. For studies addressing dual process theory and similar topics relevant to emotional decision making, please see J. D. Greene et al., "An fMRI Investigation of Emotional Engagement in Moral Judgment," *Science* 293.5537 (2001): 2105–08; Bruno B. Averbeck and Brad Duchaine, "Integration of Social and Utilitarian Factors in Decision Making," *Emotion* 9.5 (2009): 599–608; Joseph A. Mikels et al., "Should I Go With My Gut? Investigating the Benefits of Emotion-Focused Decision Making," *Emotion* 11.4 (2011): 743–753; Mathieu Cassoti et al., "Positive Emotional Context Eliminates the Framing Effect in Decision-Making," *Emotion* 12.5 (2012): 926–931. For a critical response to Greene et al. and their dual process theory, see J. Moll and R. de Oliveira-Souza, "Response to Greene: Moral sentiments and reason: friends or foes?" *Trends in Cognitive Sciences* 11.8 (2007): 323–24.

[2] For an example, see the review by Craig Anderson, "Noah Review: A Theological Void Washes Away the Heaviness of the Flood," *Bible Study and the Christian Life*, accessed 1 October 2015, https://web.archive.org/web/20141026075718.

the department, it nonetheless led to future ponderings about whether the students or faculty had thought about how to integrate faith into theatrical instruction. Is there a way to pay more than lip service to a person's faith and their art? Is praying before a performance or a rehearsal the only way to integrate faith and art? What is covered in core classes for other students getting similar degrees? Are they trained to think critically about their faith and their art, or are they taught only the techniques and skills that are learned in nearly any other state or non-faith-based school in the country? These questions form the basis for future research, and it is the intention of this study to begin the long process of finding and/or developing satisfactory answers.

The third and final reason this study holds personal significance is that the author desires to know the way that current faculty and theatre students understand their faith. This stems from a desire to teach undergraduate students who want to work in the arts, and specifically students at a Christian university. It is believed that having training in the fields of practical theology, biblical studies, and theatre will allow this author to better grasp the fundamental assumptions that students bring to their faith as it relates to their desired profession. Just as a doctor needs to know the different veins within the body, this training has brought about knowledge of different denominations, theologies, and histories within the Christian body. This knowledge, combined with the knowledge of how today's student artists understand their faith and envision it intersecting with their work, will lead to better teaching and mentoring by providing more personalized and relevant instruction.

In addition to the personal rationales for this study, as has been noted in chapter one, the literature dealing with faith integration, spiritual formation, and theatrical studies is virtually nonexistent. It largely addresses pastoral and congregational concerns, and the voices of the artists themselves are largely silent. How do theatre students and faculty themselves understand faith integration and spiritual formation happening in the sensate and tactile realm that is a theater space? Further, do these same people believe that their work is separate from their faith, or is their faith more interwoven within the various theatrical disciplines than appears at first glance? The literature is largely silent, and so this study seeks to examine whether or not the hypothesis about educational fragmentation is actually true, and to add to the literary field by providing information about lived, taught, and desired faith integration training and experiences within the narrative arts. Additionally, although this is a case study of one institution's approach to faith integration, this study can clarify what the perceived results of that integration are, and it can allow other institutions to compare their own methodologies and attempts at integration with those presented in this paper.

**Methodology: Hermeneutical Phenomenology**

So how are these various questions listed above going to be answered, and how will this study support or rebut the hypotheses presented? Put another way, what is the methodology of the study? This study is a *hermeneutical phenomenology*, a methodology that is "oriented toward lived experience and interpreting the 'texts' of life."[3]

Phenomenology is a qualitative research methodology[4] that is popular within psychology, philosophy, and certain social sciences and areas of religious studies, including practical theology, and that "describes the meaning for several individuals of the lived experiences of a concept or a phenomenon."[5] More specifically, a hermeneutical phenomenology is a study that not only describes the meaning of a concept or phenomenon, but then goes further and attempts to *interpret* that meaning. Put another way, "this description consists of 'what' they experienced and 'how' they experienced it."[6]

The title of "founding father" of phenomenology as a methodology is commonly bestowed upon Edmund Husserl (1859–1938). Desiring to break with the majority positivist orientation of philosophical thought, he believed that experience was the true source of all knowledge, and he therefore sought to create a way in which, by examining one's experiences, a person could come to know the "essence" of that experience or phenomenon.[7] Husserl's work was furthered by subsequent philosophers such as Heidegger and Sartre, and has since been utilized in numerous research fields such as psychology, sociology, social work and practical theology.[8] Because of this philosophical background and undergirding, phenomenology seeks to understand the meaning behind an experience or phenomenon that normal scientific methods could not explain or study.

Just as there are four walls to support a structure, there are four philosophical "walls" that are common supports in phenomenology. First is a desire to return to the traditional tasks of philosophy, that is, a return to the Greek conception of philosophy as a search for wisdom. This is closely connected to the next philosophical wall, which is that phenomenology should be without

---

[3] John W. Creswell, *Qualitative Inquiry & Research Design: Choosing Among Five Approaches* (2nd ed.; Thousand Oaks, CA: SAGE Publications, 2007), 59.

[4] It should be noted here that I differ slightly from the thinking of Kathleen Greider, who argues that a "methodology" is a "way to understand research" or a "discussion of methods." For her, this understanding comes from any "meta-theoretical perspectives" that are aligned with a methodology. Yet, in her view, Richard Osmer's "strategies of inquiry," which include phenomenology, are still methods that are employed within the researcher's larger conceptual framework. While I understand her point, largely for reasons of practicality I would suggest that the "strategies of inquiry" can be understood as methodologies because they bring with them inherent philosophies and presuppositions that exist as "meta-theoretical perspectives." Consequently, in this instance hermeneutical phenomenology is the methodology because it explains the philosophical approach taken in gathering and interpreting the data, whereas the methods are the practical ways in which that data was collected and disseminated. This information regarding Greider is taken from class notes, "Seminar in Practical Theology" (Claremont School of Theology, Claremont CA, September 28, 2011).

[5] Creswell, *Qualitative Inquiry*, 57.

[6] Creswell, *Qualitative Inquiry*, 58.

[7] On Husserl's thought, see "Edmund Husserl," *Standford Encyclopedia of Philosophy*: https://plato.stanford.edu/entries/husserl/ (accessed 3/9/17).

[8] According to "Qualitative Approaches," *Research Methods Knowledge Base*, last modified October 20, 2006, https://web.archive. org/web/20160124032925.

presuppositions. This suspension of judgment, called "*epoché*" by Edmund Husserl, is necessary to allow the meaning as understood by the participants to present itself without filters or preconceived notions on the part of the researcher. The third supporting wall is the intentionality of consciousness: consciousness is always directed toward an object and the reality of an object is related to one's consciousness about it. Thus, when perceiving a tree, "my intentional experience is a combination of the outward appearance of the tree and the tree as contained in my consciousness based on memory, image, and meaning."[9] Tied to this is the fourth and final wall, which is the refusal of the subject-object dichotomy. This means that the reality of an object is only perceived within the meaning of an experience of an individual.[10]

These four walls undergird the approach taken in this study. It seeks to understand *what* students and faculty experience as "faith integration" or "spiritual formation," and to know *how* they interpret a particular event, experience, person, or space in their own spiritual understanding. The study is phenomenological because (1) it searches for common wisdom among the participants, (2) it tries to suspend preconceived notions about faith integration as much as is possible so that the voices of the students and faculty can speak of their own accord, (3) it seeks to raise consciousness about faith integration and spiritual formation in the experiences of those who are teaching or learning (thus giving it a name and a "realness" that could otherwise be overlooked), and (4) it seeks to make concrete the *concept* of faith integration in the lived experiences of theatre faculty and students in order to give it meaning and a location in their practices.

Even with the intentional structure of these four walls there are, of course, some inherent biases or presuppositions in this study that need to be admitted. Though perhaps not impossible, it is extremely unlikely that any investigator can fully bracket or remove the knowledge and experiences that have brought him or her to the place where they have chosen to undertake research, and in this instance it is no different. First it must be noted that this study holds to the inherent assumption that there *is and should be* integration between a person's faith and their vocational training, and that this integration *affects the type of work produced* by these individuals. Second, as the primary investigator the author initiated contact with professional colleagues at the university where this study takes place, and was able to do so because of preexisting relationships. Because of the presence of these professional and at times personal relationships, the author has had to take extra care to bracket out any feelings of good or ill will that might exist, both toward the people and the institution involved. Though this cannot be a double-blind study, steps have been taken in order to mitigate any bias that may exist in the data analysis stage. These steps will be expanded upon later in this chapter. Third, because students are involved in the study and the author has taught collegiate courses, there has always been a possibility that a present or former student may volunteer to participate. In order to address this, no students enrolled in the author's courses during the time of

---

[9] C. Moustakas, *Phenomenological Research Methods* (Thousand Oaks, CA: SAGE Publications, 1994), 55, quoted in Creswell, Qualitative Inquiry, 235–36.

[10] This information is nicely summarized by Creswell, *Qualitative Inquiry*, 58.

data collection were allowed to participate (though this issue did not arise, for various reasons), and former students (a) had the option of interviewing with another interviewer and having their statements be transcribed by another authorized researcher, and (b) could only participate if there was no chance that this author could ever teach them again (e.g., they were graduating at the end of the data collection semester). A final example of a bias of this study is the belief that theatre arts are immensely valuable for the spiritual growth of any person of faith. Consequently, this study focuses exclusively on the relationship between the arts and faith integration, and it does not address any similar questions or concerns with respect to other academic disciplines. This may lead those involved in other disciplines to question the inherent value of the study altogether, but there is hope is that it will lead to similar studies in other disciplines in order to expand upon the data already out there.

Different researchers have different procedures and methods which they follow in order to do a phenomenological study. This study follows the general structure put forth by Max van Manen,[11] Professor Emeritus at the University of Alberta, Canada, and one of the foremost authorities on phenomenology. Van Manen understands phenomenological research to be interplay between six research activities:

(1) turning to a phenomenon which seriously interests us and commits us to the world;

(2) investigating experience as we live it rather than as we conceptualize it;

(3) reflecting on the essential themes which characterize the phenomenon;

(4) describing the phenomenon through the art of writing and     rewriting;

(5) manipulating a strong and oriented pedagogical relation to the phenomenon;

(6) balancing the research context by considering parts and whole.[12]

These six steps are not necessarily linear, and certain steps may be repeated throughout the course of the study. Further, for an endeavor such as this van Manen's step #2 must be expanded to seek understanding of both lived experience *as well as* desired experience. Knowing the *vision* or *ideals* that both faculty and students may have about how faith integration should happen in theatre might in fact lead to those visions and ideals happening, and may shed new insights on the lived experience. If a professor or student has not given much thought to faith integration, then they have no idea about the potential benefits it could offer. But if they are able to identify a vision or goal for it, then steps can be taken to implement that vision or goal and make it a reality.

---

[11] Max van Manen, *Researching Lived Experience: Human Science for an Action Sensitive Pedagogy* (2nd ed.; London, ON: State University of New York Press, 1990).

[12] Max van Manen, *Reseaching Lived Experience,* 30–31, cited in "Phenomenology as an Educational Research Method—van Manen," University of Maryland, accessed on April 17, 2011, https://web.archive.org/web/20110925065822.

In addition to van Manen's six research activities, John Creswell has also put forth some general steps that may be followed when undertaking phenomenological research. First, he states, the researcher determines if phenomenology is the proper methodology to employ. Second, a suitable topic or field of study must be found. Third, the philosophical assumptions of the methodology must be explained and the researcher must set aside his or her preconceived ideas and experiences in order to more accurately describe the participants' understandings of the phenomenon. Fourth, data are collected from the participants. Interviews are the primary method of data collection in phenomenological studies, but other material may be used as well, such as observations, journals, art, formally written responses, accounts of vicarious experiences, music, and others. Fifth, the data are analyzed using *horizontalization*, which is finding "significant statements, sentences, or quotes that provide an understanding of how the participants experienced the phenomenon."[13] From this horizontalization process *"clusters of meaning,"* or theme- or meaning-units, are then developed. With these clusters of meaning, the researcher moves to the sixth step, which is to create a *textual description*, a written description of what the participants experience. A *structural description* is also written to describe the context or setting which influenced how the participants experienced the phenomenon. Finally, the researcher writes a composite description "that presents the 'essence' of the phenomenon.... Primarily this section focuses on the common experiences of the participants."[14] Finding and describing this "essence," also referred to as the "essential, invariant structure,"[15] is the goal of the phenomenological researcher:

> to reduce the textural (*what*) and structural (*how*) meanings of experiences to a brief description that typifies the experiences of all the participants in the study. All individuals experience it; hence, it is invariant, and it is a reduction to the 'essentials' of the experiences.[16]

These seven steps put forth by Creswell, along with van Musen's six research activities, serve as a general guide for how this study has been conducted.

*Applied Method of Inquiry*

If research is like building a house, we have laid the rational and methodological foundation upon which everything else is built. Further, we have examined the four philosophical walls that support everything that happens inside the house. Now let us turn our attention to the building design. To continue the analogy, these are the rooms of the house: the *who, what, when, where, why* and *how* questions that must be fully addressed in order for a study to have validity. Each question has a different layer of complexity; some are simple like a bedroom, while others require a lot of maintenance and special accommodation in order to function properly (think of a kitchen, with all of its plumbing, venting, and electrical

---

[13] Creswell, *Qualitative Inquiry*, 61.

[14] Creswell, *Qualitative Inquiry*, 62.

[15] Creswell, *Qualitative Inquiry*, 235.

[16] Creswell, *Qualitative Inquiry*, 235 (emphasis original).

needs). But every room must be given proper attention in order for the house to meet its full intention.

In the case of this study, the *why* question has largely been addressed already. It is worth adding, though, that this study has great relevance to both the field of theatre as well as to the discipline of practical theology. From the perspective of the educational arts communities, it can allow the partner institution to hear firsthand from its faculty and students about how they are faring in attempts to inspire and promote faith integration, and it may allow other institutions to learn from the successes and challenges that come from engaging in this endeavor. From the perspective of practical theologians, this study can be valuable because it provides a window into how future professional and ecclesiastical artists are thinking about their faith and their craft now, and it can be inferred that this understanding will impact the values, morals, and perspectives portrayed in their created art once they enter into churches and the larger entertainment culture. Because of this it is important that future artists of faith engage in strong critical reflection on the practices of their faith, the practices of the Church, and the practices of the world, or, to put it another way, that they themselves become practical theologians in their own right.[17]

Like the *why* question, the *what* has also largely been answered. As stated earlier, this study seeks to answer two related questions: (1) How do students and faculty within a theatre department at a faith-based Christian university *imagine or envision* faith integration and spiritual growth occurring within their department? And (2), in what way is faith integration and spiritual growth *perceived* by these same undergraduate students as actually taking place, and what is the *intended* faith integration and spiritual growth presented by the faculty? Both questions are necessary. The second question needs to be answered in order to examine the current state of affairs within the academic field so that the first question, the imagined or future-oriented desires of people in these areas, may be better realized. You cannot reach your destination without knowing the path you have already travelled. So now, with familiar ground already afoot, let us move forward into the details of the study.

Because of the author's desire to focus on undergraduate theatre students and faculty, this study took place on the campus of a faith-based, Christian university that services an undergraduate population. In order for a university or college to participate, certain criteria had to be met:

1) The institution must have a Christian background and must either a) currently affiliate with a specific denomination, or b) have an explicitly Christian statement of faith to which all faculty and staff adhere;
2) The institution must teach undergraduate students;
3) The institution must offer an undergraduate major in theatre (or some equivalent), either as a BA or a BFA degree;
4) There must be enough students within the major(s) that a minimum of five students who have senior or end-term junior status, meaning

---

[17] Swinton and Mowat, *Practical Theology and Qualitative Research*, 6.

they have taken at least 75 percent of their required coursework for
their degree program, could participate if they so chose.

If an institution met the above criteria it would be considered for inclusion.
The initial scope of the study was going to be larger and more comparative, with the
study taking place across multiple campuses at multiple Christian universities or
colleges. However, due to restraints caused by time, funding, and life events, the
study had to be pared down and changed from a comparative study to a case study
of one university's theatre department.

There is hope, however, that a comparative study will be done in the future
that will build upon the work already done here. The university that participated in
the study was chosen for several practical reasons. First, it is in the greater Southern
California area, which is easily accessible to the author. Second, out of the various
universities that were contacted, this particular theatre department responded
promptly and with eagerness. Since they responded first, they were the first
university that the author engaged with, and when the scope of the study shifted it
seemed most reasonable to continue there and close down avenues at other schools
for the time being. Third, this particular department is one that the author had a
working relationship with, which facilitated trust in the intention of the study from
an early stage, both among some of the faculty and certain student populations. And
finally, this particular theatre department is large enough that a reasonable sample
of student responses could be had so that anonymity could be maintained.

Once the location was chosen and initial approval was granted from the
theatre department, the university's Institutional Review Board (IRB) was contacted
to notify them of the intention of studying a portion of their population. This
particular school has a very robust and thorough IRB process, and though approval
for interviewing human subjects had already been attained from Claremont School
of Theology, their IRB requested that a new proposal be submitted for their review
using their own forms and processes. This was submitted shortly after the New Year
in 2015, and expedited approval was granted approximately two weeks later.

During this time conversation had been taking place with the Chair of the
theatre department. It was arranged that a staff member, the department coordinator,
would handle all initial communication with students. This was done for two
reasons: (1) so that students could communicate directly with a familiar person
within the department if they had any questions or concerns; and (2) so that students
would receive the official invitation to participate in the study from a recognized
email address.

Once the IRB proposal had been approved, the first of four email
communications between the department coordinator and students was sent. All
student responses were first sent to the coordinator, who then forwarded them on to
the author. From there, direct email correspondence was used to set up meeting
times for face-to-face interviews. Students were also sent a digital copy of the
questions in advance so they could know what to expect during the interview, along
with a copy of the Informed Consent Form. The questions used in the study were
either written by the author of this study, or were adapted from Sherr, Huff and

Curran's study on student perceptions of integration of faith and learning.[18] The intention behind the adaptation was to build upon that previous study and be able to compare results by having a handful of identical questions.

Although the emails were sent to all theatre majors, only students who had completed at least 75 percent of their major coursework were asked to participate. This was communicated as being those of senior status or second semester juniors. Students were not directly asked about how many courses they had taken, but no students were interviewed who were not of senior or second-semester junior status.

While current students were being contacted by the department's coordinator, the author also began inquiring of theatre alumni/ae who resided within a reasonable distance from the university and/or the city of Claremont. As the study evolved from a comparative to a case study format, it was determined that a temporally longitudinal study could provide information that would assist in determining effective types of faith integration. This meant that students who had previously graduated from the department could be given a voice in the study. It was determined that only alumni/ae who had graduated with the theatre degree within the past eight years should be included. This was deemed appropriate because two-thirds of the current faculty members were teaching as far back as 2008, so there would be continuity in the experiences of current students and alumni/ae, while still allowing for some variation, since two faculty members had left and two more had started after that date.

Alumni/ae were contacted directly by the author because they were no longer students of the department. The alumni/ae who were approached about being in the study were those who were familiar either to the author, to the department coordinator, the department chair, and/or who still had some involvement with the university. Because it was assumed that there would be approximately five student participants in the study, the author sought a similar number of alumni/ae to balance out constituencies.

Further, it was determined by the author, in conjunction with the department chair, that all theatre faculty would participate in the study, a number also similar in size to the student and alumni/ae participants. Like the alumni/ae, faculty were contacted directly by the author via email or face to face. The study was explained to them, along with a statement that the study was departmentally and institutionally approved, and interview times were arranged. In the end, a total of sixteen people were interviewed for this research study: six faculty, five current students, four alumni/ae, and one additional researcher who manages a faith integration office at the university.[19]

Interviews were primarily conducted on the university campus between the end of January and the middle of May, 2015. All interviews were done in a face-

---

[18] Sherr, Huff and Curran, "Student Perceptions," 15–33.

[19] This person's comments are not included in the data presented in chapters 3–5. This is for several reasons: (1) this person requested not to be cited directly; (2) the study is focused on the university's theatre department, and this person does not work in the theatre department, so their comments were largely immaterial to the study at hand; and (3) the interview was conducted largely so that the author could procure a better understanding of how the larger university understood the integration of faith and learning, and to be made aware of any expectations placed upon the faculty.

to-face format. One faculty member requested a meeting location off-site, but all other interviews were done in faculty or department offices, theater spaces, study rooms, or public spaces on campus. Interviewees were given first choice as to the location of the interview in order to put them at ease. Every interview began with a discussion and signing of the Informed Consent Form, and all interviewees were given a paper copy of the form (in addition to the electronic copy they likely received via email) so that they could contact the author, the department chair, or the chair of the author's dissertation committee with any questions or concerns after the interview was over. All interviews were audio recorded by the author with the permission of the interviewee.

Once an interview was finished, interviewees were informed that the interview would be transcribed and summarized by the author or a research assistant. The transcription and the summary of the interview would then be sent to the interviewee for their perusal. Any follow-up questions that arose from the summary process would be included in the summary, and an interviewee would have the opportunity to respond to those questions, clarify any statements made during the interview, add any additional thoughts or comments, or ask that something not be included. Transcriptions and summaries were sent out to each interviewee approximately three to four weeks after the interview took place. Two alumni/ae interviews took longer than that due to extenuating circumstances, but all interviewees were given this opportunity to look over and respond to the data shared during the interview.

The idea of summarizing each interview arose out of a conversation with an academic colleague who has done her own qualitative research in another area. It replaced another idea, which was to provide online followup surveys for each participant, where they would be asked several questions that were nearly identical to those asked in the interview. The idea was that these online surveys would corroborate the data provided in the interviews. However, through the above-mentioned conversation it was determined that using these online surveys would possibly bother the participants because they would feel like they already answered the questions. The repetitiveness of the process might, in fact, provoke them either to not finish the survey, or to change their answers out of frustration over seemingly not being heard in the initial interview. Further, because nearly all of the questions posed in the survey would be open-ended, many of the participants, who were already busy with a full load of courses, graduation preparation, job hunting, grading, meetings, and/or other administrative duties, might simply decide it was not worth their time and never respond. So instead it was proposed that the online surveys be replaced with summaries, which would still allow for, as Creswell calls it, "member-checking" to occur.[20] Each interviewee received a summary of their interview, a document that they could examine that was shorter than the full interview transcript but that captured the main content of their answers. Summaries contained direct quotes, synopses of long answers, and the author's own thoughts and/or follow-up questions (differentiated from the interviewee's thoughts by being

---

[20] John Creswell, *Research Design: Qualitative, Quantitative, and Mixed Methods Approaches* (2nd ed.; Thousand Oaks, CA: SAGE Publications, 2003), 192.

clearly underlined). At the beginning of the summary document was a set of instructions for the participant, which explained the underlined statements and how they should respond if they so desired. Using summary documents was deemed an appropriate and useful tool for this study for several reasons. First, like the initial online survey idea, the summaries provided a place where "member-checking," intentional feedback from the participants, could be given. It afforded an opportunity for an interviewee to read some of their own thoughts and reflect on them, and then affirm them; amend them; and/or ask that a sentence, paragraph, or train of thought be excluded from the data pool. Thus their answers were still their own, even after they had been recorded and transcribed. Second, the summaries provided a way to check for the internal validity of the data. Original answers could be compared with any alterations, clarifications, or addendums that the interviewee might make or ask for, and discrepancies could be identified. Third, it provided a way for this author to verify some early interpretations of the data and ensure they fit with the original intention of the interviewees. Finally, the summaries served as an early step in the coding process, allowing certain themes or patterns to emerge that could then guide the more formal coding steps that followed.

After all of the interviews were completed, and after either a summary was returned by an interviewee, or a reasonable amount of time (approximately one month) had elapsed after an interviewee was sent the summary and transcription of their interview but had not returned it, the interview data (both transcription and summary) went through a coding process. Within qualitative research, such as the research project being done here, a code generally refers to "a word or short phrase that symbolically assigns a summative, salient, essence-capturing and/or evocative attribute for a portion of language-based or visual data."[21] Those who had not responded to their summary document were sent a second email, reminding them to please check the document and reply within two weeks. Those who had responded went directly into the formal coding process, where "code" words or phrases were extracted from the summaries in the hopes of understanding the essence of what was being said. This process was modeled on Creswell's concepts of "horizontalization" and clusters of meaning: each interview transcript and summary (with or without additional comments or input on the part of the interviewee) was dissected for significant statements, quotes, or concepts. Items were deemed significant if they were repeated more than once in an interview or if they appeared in transcripts or summaries from other participants. From there, items were placed into "clusters of meaning," groups with similar themes, statements, or concepts. Finally, out of these clusters of meaning grew both textual and structural descriptions.

As has been stated by research authorities, there is no "best" way to code qualitative data.[22] For this study, coding was done as a multistep process. First, the author reviewed each individual interview transcript and summary to identify significant statements, quotes, or concepts. These were listed in a running

---

[21] Johnny Saldaña, *The Coding Manual for Qualitative Researchers* (Thousand Oaks, CA: SAGE Publications, 2009), 2.

[22] Saldaña, *Coding*, 2.

spreadsheet as they were discovered. The coded data within each transcript and summary were then examined for patterns. Items that were identified as part of a pattern by the researcher were highlighted for coding inclusion and evaluated on a case by case basis.

Once this initial coding phase was complete, items from an individual interview that were chosen for inclusion in the coding process were then placed into larger categories. This allowed the author to see broader patterns in a particular interview. This process was repeated for each interview. Once all interview data had been examined, categories were reexamined to see which categories crossed boundaries between interviewees. New, larger clusters of meaning were formed, into which various categories were subsumed or refined. Finally, once these clusters of meaning were formed, textual and structural descriptions were drawn up in order to try to explain the data results. *Textual descriptions* are written descriptions of what the participants of the study experienced with regard to faith integration and/or spiritual formation. *Structural descriptions* are also written descriptions that describe the context or setting which influenced how the participants experienced the phenomenon.[23] These descriptions can be found in the next chapter, and it is to these descriptions, and the findings of this research, that we now turn.

---

[23] Creswell, *Qualitative Inquiry*, 60.

# Research Findings
## Students and Alumni/ae

Textual and structural descriptions arise from a thorough analysis of the data at hand. They are, in effect, one- to two-sentence summaries of what was experienced by the participants who were studied. But in order to understand these summaries, first the data itself must be explicated and examined. This chapter presents the data that was gathered, demonstrates the major categories or clusters of meaning that arose, and from these develops rich descriptions that capture the essence of what was experienced.

The next three chapters will be structured in the following way: first will be a short description of what the author *expected* to find. This expectation was largely drawn from personal experience and from textual research done before the implementation of the study. Following this will begin an explanation of the actual findings of the study. Though the study was conducted with three distinct population groups (current students, alumni/ae, and faculty), the rest of this chapter will focus on data derived from current students and alumni/ ae only. Faculty results will be disseminated in chapter four. Though there were some differences between what was shared by the current students and alumni/ae, these differences were negligible enough to postpone discussion of them until chapter five. At that time the process of comparing and combining data from the three populations into one larger pool that highlights the points of commonality and points of difference will take place. Finally, out of all of that analysis will arise descriptions that seek to capture the essence of the data and answer the research questions posed in early chapters.

### Expected Findings

Qualitative research rarely goes according to plan. Expectations of how long a study should take, the acquisition of permissions to do the study, the processes of finding or recruiting participants, the ease (or lack thereof) of gathering usable data, and the process of analyzing data and discovering patterns that are consistent with the truthful presentations of the people being studied all present variables that are far messier than merely examining static texts or statistics. Thus it was of little surprise that there were differences between what the author expected to find and what was actually discovered. These expectations were largely derived from personal experiences and from textual research done before the study commenced.

The personal experiences mentioned here were derived from observations and direct encounters during the author's time working in theatre, both professionally and in educational settings. From time spent as an undergraduate theatre practitioner, the author had the general conclusion that, if his experience was normative, most theatre departments at faith-based universities and colleges were not doing as good of a job integrating faith and learning as they might believe. He suspected that the efficacy of faith integration assignments was minimal, and that students were leaving the confines of their institutions and entering into the entertainment world unprepared for the challenges and moral ambiguities that they would face. It was further suspected that most faculty who taught in these types of institutions would be unaware of how spiritual formation, was happening within their department, if at all, and that this lack of awareness would lead to false assumptions or missed opportunities for faith integration to occur.

From time spent as a professional theatre employee the author surmised that even if many of the practitioners of the craft were self-professing Christians, any and all efforts at the integration of faith and continued learning were understood to be the responsibility of the individual. Discussions of faith might come up occasionally in an early rehearsal, assuming the play content lent itself to such conversation, but generally speaking, one's own personal faith direction was one's own. The journey was largely a solo one, and faith was a Sunday-morning subject. When faith was expressed it was largely through moments of personal kindness, forgiving an error, or the occasional group prayer; it was understood to be an *atmosphere* of Christ-likeness that would draw people in, with the hope that (if it existed) it may lead to conversations outside of traditional work, rehearsal, or performance times.

From time spent as a technical director for a university theatre department, the author suspected that the most influential integration of faith and learning (IFL) in a student's undergraduate experience would be through informal, personal interactions with those whom she or he respected. Though these persons would likely be faculty members, they could also be staff or peers, anyone perceived to be in a position of experiential superiority to the student. It was suspected that personal experience, stories from others, and stories learned while rehearsing a production would be the most influential, more so than an in-class assignment, because of the nature of theatrical learning and the people who are attracted to it. Just as a psychologist might naturally look at familial history and stressors to diagnose a patient, so a storyteller naturally looks toward the narrative to explain the *hows* and *whys* of life.

Finally, from time spent teaching both undergraduate theatre and nontheatre students alike, the author suspected that the placement of self into a story would be of significant influence in the life of an undergraduate theatre student. As in the story of Saint Genesius, the influence of embodied storytelling on the actor cannot be overstated.[1] The author often uses an assignment in one of his regularly taught classes that requires students to act out a modern retelling of a Biblical story. Adapted from David Torbett,[2] the assignment is a group project that requires each group to pick one of five Biblical stories and "re-set" it in a modern-day context. They have to do research on the story using commentaries and Bible dictionaries (which are new sources of information for many of them), and they have to rehearse together over a period of one to two months. Then they have to perform their

---

[1] Dan Cawthon, "The Genesian Effect: Performing Damien Deepens an Actor's Faith," *Catholic Theatre and Drama: Critical Essays* (ed. Kevin J. Wetmore, Jr.; Jefferson, NC: McFarland & Company, 2010), 209.

[2] Torbett, "'I Did Not Wash My Feet,'" 307–19.

dramatic retelling for the class, gather class feedback, and write a short paper that analyzes the story and the overall experience of doing the project. The assignment has fostered incredible conversation and feedback from students over the years. Though students are often nervous about the project, afterwards they are overwhelmingly positive and grateful for the learning opportunity, usually commenting that they had heard or read the Biblical story many times before but discovered new knowledge about it and about themselves by enacting it in a contemporary context. To borrow a reference from Peter Pitzele's *Scripture Windows*, they discover the "white fire" of interpretation around the "black fire" of the written words.[3] This type of embodied learning, particularly through acting, was another aspect of IFL that I expected to discover in the interviews, particularly those conducted with the students.

So what was found? As referenced in chapter two, this study was conducted with three distinct people groups: current students, alumni/ae, and full-time faculty within the theatre department. Because there were overwhelming points of similarity among the data collected from the current students and the alumni/ae, their data will be discussed together here. Where differences arose they will be addressed, but a more thorough discussion of why these differences exist will be postponed until chapter five. Faculty data will be presented as a separate section from the students and alumni/ae for two reasons. First, the research questions posed in this study seek information regarding student and faculty perceptions and ideals of IFL. Consequently, in order to answer those questions the data from each group must remain distinct. Second, because students and faculty have different roles in a collegiate setting, the data presented demonstrates the understood function and responsibility of each group. For example, the faculty understand their position to be one of knowledge conveyance: they take information gleaned from their own studies and experiences and use it to instruct and provide students with opportunities to use that information in their own professional maturation process. Students, on the other hand, understand their role as that of knowledge assimilation: they come to class or rehearsal prepared to be taught and challenged because their instructors want them to be prepared to work and succeed in the entertainment industry, and they assume that their directors and professors know how to make that dream a reality. Each role (faculty or student) naturally is going to have different assumptions about what faith integration is, how to use it, where it might be found, and why it is important. Thus it is for these two reasons, the purpose of this study and the roles of the study participants, that these two groups will be examined separately. With this explanation in mind then, let us turn our attention to the students and alumni/ae of the theatre program in question.

---

[3] The full quote is: "There is a traditional Jewish commentary that talks about the Bible as having been composed in black and white fire. The black fire is seen in the form of the printed or handwritten words in the page or scroll; the white fire is found in the spaces between and around the black. The black fire is fixed for all time; the white fire is forever kindled by fresh encounters between changing times and the unchanging words. The black fire establishes the canonized object we can all see before us; the white spaces represent the endless potential for the fresh interpretation of that object." Pitzele, *Scripture Windows*, 23–24.

**Actual Findings: Students and Alumni/ae**

Most theatre departments at evangelical Christian colleges and universities are not large. Though there does not appear to be any official survey data publicly available, conversations with a dozen overtly Christian universities across the country provide evidence that there was an average of 38 students in any given program, with a high of 90 and a low of 10.[4]

The educational institution where the author's research took place has a theatre major with a student population of 75–100 students. It has a higher percentage of freshmen and sophomores than it does juniors and seniors. Factoring out those who were ineligible to be a part of this study because of their academic standing (i.e., they did not have senior or secondsemester junior academic status), there were 34 students who *could* have chosen to participate. Out of that number, five expressed interest in the study and four contacted the author to set up an interview appointment. Though a larger number of current students would have been preferable, a sample size of 12 percent allowed me to gain some understanding of current views on IFL and influences on spiritual formation. In part due to the relatively small sample size, it was deemed prudent to seek out alumni/ae of the program who would be willing to participate in the study as well. In order to maintain some level of consistency in the study, alumni/ae had to have taken classes with at least four of the six current faculty members and have graduated with a theatre degree. This led to five additional alumni/ae participants, which brought the research to a level of saturation that was deemed sufficient by the researcher and his committee to adequately answer the questions being posited in the study.

In order to maintain the promised anonymity to the students and alumni/ae who participated, for the purposes of this study the four students will be identified as S1, S2, S3, and S4, and the five alumni/ae will be identified as A1, A2, A3, A4, and A5. General demographic data of these groups is as follows.

Of the current students, 3 were female and 1 was male; 3 were straight and 1 was gay; 2 were Anglo, 1 was Latino/a, and 1 was black; and 2 were academic seniors and 2 were second-semester academic juniors.

Of the alumni/ae, 2 were male and 3 were female; all 5 were straight; and 4 were Anglo and 1 was Hispanic. All graduated between 2007–2012.

This data is not presented sequentially in order to preserve their anonymity (e.g., S1 and S2 are not necessarily straight, Anglo females who were seniors, and A1 is not necessarily a straight Anglo male).

---

[4] This data was collected by the author and his research assistant. All twelve schools had statements of faith, were Protestant in history and practice, and generally could be categorized as being conservative and/or evangelical. The college with the smallest number of theatre majors (ten students) had just stopped admitting students to the major and had eliminated the program altogether. Two of the most robust programs offer multiple degrees (e.g., a BA and a BFA) within their respective departments. Most schools offered a theatre minor, which increased enrollment in theatre courses (for example, one school had thirty-five majors and nineteen minors, which increases the degree headcount by 54 percent).

All of the students and alumni/ae stated that the integration of faith and theatrical learning was beneficial, and all nine self-identified as persons of faith. How they each defined "person of faith" varied somewhat, however.

S1 stated that it involved trusting in God and having a relationship with Him; S2 also referenced the personal relationship with God, but added "following Him" as a key component of that relationship; S3 stated that she believed in Jesus and thought there needed to be a "practicing" element of faith, such as attending church and/or having accountability in order for faith to grow and mature; and S4 felt that faith was very personal to each person (a "thumbprint") and involved recognizing one's own humanity, which was defined as "realizing that you're not God," that a person answers to God, and that a person can "put trust in" God. S4 did admit though that he did not have a "fully developed sense of what my faith is and means to me." Throughout the course of each conversation it became clear that of the four students, two had what this researcher would describe as a mature faith (e.g., presented articulately, well reasoned, and showing evidence of an integrated worldview), one was in a "complacent state" about faith but had the knowledge, and one was wrestling with Christian identity and the application of faith.

For the alumni/ae population, A1 believed a person of faith to be someone who has accepted Jesus Christ as Savior, has a relationship with Him, and has accepted grace. A2 focused more on the effect of being a person of faith, stating that it defined her worldview and her mission in life, as well as how she made decisions. She also felt it important that a person of faith participate in a church body. A3 also spoke about a relationship with Jesus Christ, but spoke more about having faith in "God's provision," which was understood to mean that God will provide, test people, and help in tough situations; will not give more to a person than they can handle, and is in control of all things. A4 understood a person of faith to believe that God exists, creates, and has a purpose for humanity. Her faith in particular also helped her deal with rejection in the industry, a concept that will be addressed later in the data. And finally, A5 defined a person of faith as someone who applies the teachings of Jesus to daily life and to their actions. Throughout the course of each conversation it was evident that of the five alumni/ae, four had what this researcher would describe as a mature faith (e.g., presented articulately, well reasoned, and showing evidence of an integrated worldview), and one had a faith that that was integrated into a Christian worldview but which they had a difficult time articulating.

During the transcription and coding stages of the research it became clear that there were numerous ways in which these students and alumni/ae were influenced in their own spiritual growth. These influences and the ways they were described provided illumination as to how they perceived effective IFL. In no particular order, one such way that came to the forefront, and that can be classified as our first cluster of meaning within the student and alumni/ ae population, was the role of faculty as *mentors*.

*Mentors*

Three of the four students mentioned *mentors* as influential in their spiritual lives, as did all five alumni/ae. These were always faculty members as opposed to fellow students, and the type of mentoring varied depending on the context of the conversation. Two of the four students, and two of the five alumni/ae, alluded to what we will refer to as "intentional mentoring," which for our purposes will refer to a style of mentoring that follows the traditional model where two or more people plan intentional meeting times to discuss and work through areas of life.

In intentional mentoring, one or more persons (the mentees) are usually younger and the other (the mentor) is older. They are often brought together because of some point of commonality, where the mentor has some knowledge, skill, or wisdom that the younger mentee finds desirable and wishes to learn. This relationship could be established by either party and lasts for as long as all participants wish. The purpose of this mentoring is to engage the entirety of the person in order to bring about personal and social awareness, with the intention that this awareness will lead to growth and maturity. It places both the mentor and mentee in a community of openness and grace.

> Spiritual formation is rooted in relationship with God and with one another. Communities of grace and trust help us discover and define who we are and how we shall live in trust, love, grace, humility, dignity, and justice. Communities of grace and trust open the door to gaining permission to share truth among fellow believers and the unbelieving world.[5]

It is worth noting here that intentional mentoring can often happen in group settings, especially among evangelical Christians who determine to study the Bible together. The author has known professors and staff members who have led Bible studies and times of prayer for any students who are interested. Many times these may be gender-specific in order to make the setting more comfortable and open. One example is a professor at the university studied here who discipled a group of female theatre students. They set up meeting times to read through the Bible or go through a Bible study, pray together, and talk about issues of life. While this was not a one-on-one context, it constitutes traditional mentoring because of the nature of the relationship between this professor and the students: the professor, as the elder woman with the most life experience, had arranged it so that the students could learn from her mistakes and triumphs and apply that knowledge to their own lives.

The location for intentional mentoring is primarily within the general campus life. While it may occur in either the classroom or production setting of a theatre department, this is both unlikely and unwise. Within the classroom there are inherent power dynamics: if a teacher is both "objectively" grading a student *and* mentoring him/her, there is a conflict of interest. Also, the student may feel compelled, either from internal assumptions or external signs, to modify the content of the mentoring relationship in order to appease the mentor/teacher and achieve a reward (e.g., a good grade). Within the production setting it is also unlikely to find traditional mentoring due to the many pressing needs placed upon those people who would most likely be in a mentoring position, such as directors or producers: if a

---

[5] Alan Andrews, ed., *The Kingdom Life: A Practical Theology of Discipleship and Spiritual Formation* (Colorado Springs: NavPress, 2010), 18.

director needs to get through a certain number of scenes, then pragmatically speaking s/he is not going to have the *time* to engage in intentional mentoring.

In the context of this study the intentional mentor, who was always a faculty member, served as a "guide" for the student. S2 referred to a particularly influential faculty member as someone who has "your best interest at heart. And you're a part of their life and their mind and their prayers, not just for that hour and a half [in the classroom] but for the entire time you're here." This faculty member "attempt[s] to understand you" and was open to knowing S2 deeply as a person, not just as a student in the classroom. S4 spoke of an adjunct professor who was willing to be at their "disposal if I ever needed her," even outside of the university environment and after their graduation. Similarly, among the alumni/ae population intentional mentors were spoken of highly.

A2 had a faculty mentor who was "very, very formative" and with whom she

> would meet regularly, probably about every other week, and just pray together, sometimes read Scripture and just talk about questions that I had. So that was also very formative to me as well, as she demonstrated just someone who had been through a lot of the same things that I had and struggled with a lot of the same questions and didn't look down on me or, like, or patronize me for having certain questions or struggles, but would be in those moments with me and also point me towards... point me in the direction of Christ and point me towards resources, [such as] Scriptures, books, [or] pray for me or things.

As this quote illustrates, the role of an intentional mentor was highly influential in the lives of those students who had one. A5, though she did not have an intentional mentor of her own, referred to "one-on-one mentoring" as almost essential for professors who want to "really know" the spiritual dynamic of their students. "They'd have to... really seriously take the time to meet with me, and to read between the lines of assignments and such." Thus intentional mentoring, though not available for all students or alumni/ae, was understood to be an important part of the spiritual growth of a student and a tangible way in which faith integration was expressed.

The second type of mentoring that was apparent was what will be referred to as "*in situ* mentoring," or informal, situation-specific mentoring. This occurs in everyday situations as people are in class together, rehearsing together, or simply engaged in casual conversation. Unlike intentional mentoring, *in situ* mentoring can easily take place in any number of arenas because it is not formally planned: the classroom, a production, or in general campus life. Within the classroom setting, this style of mentoring may appear very similar to standard teacher/student models. However, based on student and alumni/ae interviews it seems the most impactful when it happens in small-group settings or even one-on-one situations. It should also be noted that many of the theatre classes referenced by the participants in this study are small by most undergraduate standards, usually ranging from 10–20 students, and therefore *in situ* mentoring may happen more easily. Further, because of the participatory nature of many theatre classes, *in situ* mentoring may happen more frequently than in other fields.

Student S2 referred to a top-rated professor[6] who made faith applicable to "where you're at in life," which required great personal knowledge on the part of the professor about the student in question. Student S3 discussed another highly rated professor who created a healthy working environment in her classroom. The professor discussed how "intentional we should be about dealing with 'dark' or 'heavy' material, and how it can be unbelievably vulnerable and touching and revealing to human nature if done well, but can be very scarring and dangerous if not." And like their younger counterparts, alumni/ae also spoke of *in situ* mentors as being examples of faith integration in their classes: A1 had professors who were willing to sit and talk personally with her, and even go so far as to personalize their teaching methods to her learning style; A2 had a professor who was "academic" in her teaching style but still made herself "available for [faith] conversations"; A4 stated that a professor who cared about the spiritual growth of students would engage with student projects in a class in order to gauge their spiritual maturity and awareness, and she listed a top-rated professor who always created a "nurturing" atmosphere in their classroom, which fostered these very things; and A5 gave an example of *in situ* mentoring where a professor spoke of her own experiences where she made the wrong choice in an ethical decision, and admonished her students to think through their own stances to various moral dilemmas. Interestingly, A5 referred to all faculty as "mentors" whether they felt they were or not, or "whether or not there was ever any conversation about it."

*In situ* mentoring also occurred during production work. In her book *Stanislavsky in Focus*, Sharon Carnicke explains two different acting styles that came from the famous Russian acting instructor and director, Konstantin Sergeevich Stanislavsky.[7] One style, which became known as the Strasburg Method, focuses almost exclusively on the emotions of the actor. The other style, the Method of Physical Actions style (or Adler Method), focuses more on the circumstances of the play's story and how they affect the character. Both schools are important and both can be effective, but their effectiveness is largely dependent upon the personality and needs of the actor; certain actors work better with one style or the other. In the same manner, certain actors may respond to various spiritual techniques or insights more readily than others. *In situ* mentoring in production work can be effective because it can provide a space where personal spiritual needs can be addressed within fluid and natural settings that relate to theatrical needs. Student S4 spoke at length about a director who helped him recognize and realize his potential and ability as an actor. "She understood where I was coming from. It was a perfect example of someone seeing something in you that you couldn't see and being able to just kind of draw it out of you and work with you and not give up on you because they have that faith in you." As this quote illustrates, S4 received personal attention and guidance from the director that connected his acting ability with his faith. This

---

[6] One question posed to all students and alumni/ae asked them to rank three professors on a scale of 1–10, where 1 is the lowest and 10 is the highest, based on their efforts to integrate faith and learning in the classroom. From here on out any reference to a "ranked" professor (e.g., "top ranked" or "lowest ranked") refers to this question.

[7] Sharon M. Carnicke, *Stanislavsky in Focus* (1998; repr., London: Harwood Academic Publishers, 2003).

attention was very meaningful for him and references to this director and her role as a mentor in S4's life were found all throughout the interview.

Similarly, just as production settings can be a catalyst for *in situ* mentoring, so too can informal meetings. These may take place in cafeterias, unscheduled office visits, or hallways around campus. Because of the familiarity that students and faculty have with each other in theatre departments, fostered in no small part because of the extensive and varied ways in which they interact (e.g., classes, rehearsals, travels, projects), these meetings can have the same type of effect as production *in situ* mentoring. A1 mentioned a production staff member (who had a role not unlike some faculty) who provided encouragement, prayer, and advice for her after the breakup of a long relationship. A4 spoke about a professor who would check in with her outside of classes and productions to make sure she was doing alright and to offer a listening ear or a supportive shoulder. And A5 reflected back on faculty who were "invested" in his spiritual growth by their presence and care for his overall wellbeing. Overall, three of the four students referred to *in situ* mentoring in their interviews, and all five of the alumni/ae spoke of situations where it was present as a positive influence in their own lives as well.

*Modeling*

The second cluster of meaning that arose from the interviews was the influence of faculty *modeling*. In some fashion, all nine participants spoke of faculty models as being highly influential in their spiritual journeys during their time at university. In fact, out of all of the clusters of meaning, modeling had the greatest point of commonality among the participants, and there were nearly 40 points of identification within the four student interviews and over 50 points among the five alumni/ae interviews where modeling was implied or stated. There is a lot of overlap between modeling and mentoring, but the primary distinction between the two areas rests in the fact that, whereas mentoring requires intentional instruction and investment in the lives of students by a faculty member, modeling can exist where the modeler has no awareness of its affect on those who witness it.[8] Modeling, though it can be (and often is) intentional, may be done out of a place of ignorance. Because of this, modeling often reflects more of the actual character of the modeler than mentoring. Further, whereas a mentor can speak about something and leave it at that, modeling requires the actual *doing* of something. A mentor might, for example, advise a student not to take a role in a play because of moral concerns, but they may not have ever faced that particular dilemma themselves. A model, on the other hand, would have faced a similar situation in the past that informs their advice, and/or they would simply be observed rejecting a role for stated reasons that resonated with one or more people who witnessed it.

There were several types of modeling referenced by the students and alumni/ae. Each type had its own distinctive characteristics that made it different from the others, but there were also a number of similarities between several types of modeling that made it difficult to identify and categorize them. However, in order

---

[8] "Affect" is used here intentionally, as modeling often brought about a true change in the life of the student or alumni/ae. They were affected, and their consequent spiritual growth was the effect.

to develop a thick and rich description of modeling, the author found it necessary to nuance descriptions where appropriate in order to most accurately reflect the intentions of the participants.

The first type of modeling is *decision making*. Broadly speaking, decision making in this context refers to the intentional inclusion of faith and spirituality in the various decisions that a person (or persons) faces daily. Its purpose is to model submission to God's purposes and desires, and it requires considerable self-awareness and spiritual maturity on the part of the person who does it. It requires self-awareness because the person must know their limitations, understand the broader issue being considered, and be aware of the ramifications of their decision. It requires spiritual maturity because this type of modeling can be very humbling: it often acknowledges a lack of knowledge, worth, or ability on the part of the model, and a reliance on God's direction. It also implies that the modeler is spiritually mature enough and capable of understanding a directive from God regarding the particular decision that needs to be made.

Three of the four students cited examples of decision making that were influential in some way. For several of them this decision making happened when a professor chose the play or musical that was going to be a part of their season for the year. S1 referenced a show that had a lot of "morality on the outside" and was "Christian," which made it easier to see how it related to her faith. S3 cited an influential director who modeled a "faith-centered approach to the show." For others, such as S2, the decision related to how the professors chose to understand the purpose of art: "they have this way of being able to intellectually describe and pull you into this idea of truth, and God is truth." In the eyes of these professors, as interpreted by S2, it is not the job of the actor to morally correct another's story, but rather to tell it truthfully. By telling it truthfully, one learns that there is "beauty in brokenness," and that there are also "capital 'T' Truths" that are God's Truths and cannot not be Truths. These Truths find their way into all stories, including those that are not overtly faithbased. "And so if you're telling a story with these Truths of struggle, of pain, of hurt... in that way you can see threads of faith all throughout it, [so that people] can so evidently see God's hand and things pointing to God and pointing to faith and grace and all of these things that are fundamental to faith." Finally, both S2 and S3 made clear that a professor who simply had a "Christ-centered mindset" (S3) and who approached topics from a faith perspective was modeling faithful decision making. For S3 in particular, the attitude of the professor toward IFL was very important. While not the only factor, "the success of faith integration starts with the instructor." Indeed, a professor's ability to keep faith and theatrical practices together was directly connected to their perceived care for students' spiritual growth.

For the alumni/ae, the modeling of decision making was referenced by all five participants, an indicator that this type of modeling was understood to be very significant. A1 listed an example of IFL in a production where the director modeled Christian leadership by "showing right and wrong behavior," demonstrated through her decision to "not tolerate" unprofessional "drama going on backstage.... And I really appreciated that." A2 spoke of a professor who shared their decisions related to struggles in life, and how those decisions modeled a spiritually integrous life. A3 incorporated the modeling of decision making into his ideal understanding of IFL in both classroom and production settings, speaking reverently of a professor who conducted her class in such a manner that she could share personal stories and tell students about decisions she had made that related to her own spiritual walk, and who chose shows that could "open the door" for conversations about faith. Both of these examples modeled decision making in an ideal way for this alumnus, and seeing how this professor expressed matters of faith through her choices emboldened him to be forthright about his own faith in the decisions he has faced as well. Like A3, A4 also believed that choosing plays that can "enrich faith" was part of the ideal faith integration, and A5 saw the demonstration of faith through actions and choices as ideal for the classroom.

The second type of modeling that was brought to light from the interviews was *interpersonal modeling*. All four students affirmed that interpersonal modeling, that is, the way a model interacted with those around him or her, was very influential in the way they perceived faith integration and/or grew in their own faith. Each student was asked to rate three professors on a scale of 1–10 based on their efforts to integration faith and learning, and one of the top-rated professors for S2 received a 10 because they[9] were a "walking example." S3 described a good professor as being "empathetic," "compassionate," and "understanding." And S4 spoke of a professor who was patient with him and "understood where I was coming from. It was a perfect example of someone seeing something in you that you couldn't see and being able to just kind of draw it out of you and work with you and not give up on you because they have that faith in you." In perhaps the greatest example of interpersonal modeling, S1 spoke of a professor who spent 30–40 minutes working one-on-one with her during a class in order to help her break through a barrier in her personal and professional life. "She [the professor] stayed with me the entire time. And she was relentless, but she was also gentle. She wasn't berating me..., but she was telling, you know, 'You have to get over it or else... you're not going to be ready to leave [the university and go out as a professional].'... So yeah... professors care." As these examples show, interpersonal modeling can happen in a classroom or in a production, and exhibits characteristics (e.g., empathy, compassion) that imply that it can easily exist in other settings as well. Further, though it is often a part of the instructional capacity of the faculty position it may appear in more casual conversation or encounters.

For the alumni/ae in the study, interpersonal modeling appeared in four of the five interviews. A1 spoke at length about professors who were willing to pray for her and who wanted to know about her life. They provided examples to her of "Christian leadership" because of their care and shared interests, and a part of this "leadership" modeling was how they interacted with her. Also, A1 stated that a professor who disrespected their students hurt their efforts at achieving effective IFL, whereas a professor who modeled grace and encouragement to students and showed them respect was effective. For A2, interpersonal modeling occurred when her highest-rated professor discussed why "living out [our faith]... was so important." Like A1, whereas a professor who would "dismiss or belittle a student's

---

[9] S2 chose to not identify this particular professor, so the gender is unknown.

49

question or concern about… how their faith fit into their field or… their life" was ineffective in their attempts at faith integration, an effective approach to IFL was one that acknowledged the student and their question, even if that question was not answered at that time. "When a student has the courage to bring up something that they've been thinking about… I think it should be acknowledged, and if it can't be talked about at that very moment… then [later it can be] followed through." For A2, the interpersonal relationship that a faculty member had with a student, simply through acknowledging them, was understood to be more important than the content of the conversation itself. For A3, the ideal IFL in a classroom setting was one where the professor interacted with students in a courteous and professional way because their faith was lived out through their actions. And like A1 and A2, A3 felt that if a professor's disregard for a student was understood to be a negative factor in their efforts at IFL, then the expression of care for a student through acknowledgement and listening to that student was seen as critical to faith integration expression. Finally, A5 spoke about moments in his collegiate career where he witnessed "underhandedness" that promoted "drama and competition" among members of the department, and contrasted these professors with many others who set a "good example" of interpersonal kindness and consideration. This contrast provided what he termed "points of consideration," which led to conscious thinking about interpersonal behavior and the spiritual dynamics of interpersonal encounters.

Closely related to interpersonal modeling is the third type of modeling, *valuing*, and like interpersonal, all four students and four of the five alumni/ae indicated that valuing was significant in their understanding of positive faith integration. Valuing refers to the way a model shows the worthiness (value) of another person or people through the way they treated them. This is obviously very closely connected to interpersonal modeling, in that the most effective interpersonal models are those who acknowledge and appreciate the value in others, but a person can demonstrate interpersonal skills without acknowledging the value of the other. In a professional relationship, for example, one person might value the inherent knowledge of the other regarding a particular subject, but valuing knowledge is not the same as valuing the person.

In this study the four student participants referenced some instance or type of valuing well over a dozen times. For S1, the ideal valuing in a theatrical context would exhibit open-mindedness and understanding of the other (a sentiment echoed by S4). Interestingly, however, although these ideals were spoken of in the abstract by S1, there were no concrete examples of "open mindedness" or "understanding" among the professors that she mentioned, even though some of them were rated and/or spoken of very highly. In fact, the only direct reference to professors modeling valuing was a statement about how they (the general theatre department faculty) "love all of us. That doesn't necessarily mean that we all have good relationships with all of them, you know, some people have gotten into arguments, but I think that they all care about us. And I know that that's commonly said at schools and different things. 'I'm your teacher, I love you,' and all this, 'I care about you.' But I truly do see that here at [University]." This valuing, expressed as care, seems to imply that this student's experience of valuing was different than how she thought it should ideally be expressed.

In an interesting contrast, S2 spoke of the ideal valuing as being nonjudgmental and that she had experienced it firsthand. "I would say the teachers who have impacted me the most are those who don't even remotely come close to judging you. That no matter what you've chosen, what mistakes you've made, where you're trying to figure things out, whether you're a mess at the moment or maybe you've kind of got things together for the time being, they never judge you. They never judge you for being too good or too bad." While this is similar to S1 (and S4), the contrast arises in that her experience matches her ideal: her relationship with her top-rated professor was one of no judgment or pressure, and she felt that this person instead tried to know and understand her. Her second-highest rated professor also valued her, and this value was demonstrated through the assumption that S2 was intelligent enough to grapple with difficult or large ideas. Her ideas were taken seriously by this professor, and as a consequence S2 felt valued. S3 also spoke of an influential professor who was encouraging, respectful, and a good listener, which fostered growth and development of the students, and S4 personalized it by speaking of a professor who was loving and caring, and helped him see his potential. Thus it seems, for three of the four students at least, the ideal type of valuing matched the experiences they had with at least one faculty member.

As an interesting side note, S3 showed great appreciation for faculty who valued IFL itself. For her, a good professor was one who would never "take lightly or disregard what faith can be integrated into what we're doing, and [would never] just write theatre off as a secular art, because it doesn't have to be a secular art." Thus her ideal valuing, at least in part, had as much to do with *what* was being valued as the act of valuing itself.

For the four alumni/ae who spoke about valuing, the results were similar to those of the students. A1 described professors who cared for students and respected them, both intellectually and spiritually. Her co-top-rated professor "leads in a way that's encouraging to her students," and the other co-top-rated professor was invested in her "wellbeing and truly the faith of the students who he encountered." A2 and A3 both said that the ideal expression of IFL in a production setting included being caring, generous, and kind to others (or to quote the words of Jesus, "love your neighbor as yourself"). Also, when speaking about her mentor, A2 referred to the "genuine care" that was expressed for her. This care made her feel valued as an individual. Similarly, A3 gave an example of a top-rated professor who "puts others before herself constantly," put her "own mental and physical wellbeing ahead of others," and exemplified a servant's heart, which gave value to him and his classmates and showed the faith of the faculty member. This selflessness was understood to be for "the good of something better," that is, the students' spiritual and professional growth. Finally, one of A4's top-rated professors modeled valuing through the tone they brought to the classroom. They modeled valuing "because they established an atmosphere in the classroom where they knew you by name, and their character [shone through], and the way they carried themselves proved that they would not just see you as a student but as a person. You know, like, that you had a purpose in that classroom in that time, and what we were studying was relevant to my life and would be." Because she was not just a mind in a seat in the classroom, but was seen as a whole "person," A4 felt valued.

The fourth type of modeling that was spoken of by the students and alumni/ae was *organic* modeling. Organic modeling refers to two components of the modeler: first, the model demonstrates a personal integrity between his or her faith and the way that they live; and second, that integrity leads to an organic, unforced expression of their faith in how they think, act, and interact with others. As with interpersonal modeling, all four students described organic modeling as being a key characteristic of a person who successfully integrates faith and learning. Two of the students explicitly stated that organic modeling was part of the ideal way for faith integration to occur within a class or production setting. Two of the students also stated that organic modeling was evidence that a professor was interested in their own faith journeys. When asked if professors were interested in her faith, S2 responded this way:

> Professors, I know absolutely are. Because they've gone through this industry with faith, and some of them have gone through part of it without faith, so they know both sides to the story. And they know how hard the industry is, period. But to do it without faith is so much harder than to do it with faith. And so to them that's hugely important, which makes them invest in us all the more because they want us to have that, obviously, if we want it as well. And so that comes across through life talks in class, outside of class, in general. But even with approaching materials specifically in our work and everything like that, because, yeah, the closer you can get to the heart of God the closer you can get to the heart of a person in my opinion, because you start to see them through a lens of love, which is how we should approach all roles.

Similarly, two other students spoke of their top-rated professors as modeling organic faith integration. S4's top professor shared her own struggles and experiences of being a person of faith in the industry, and S1 stated,

> Another [professor] I'm thinking of, she gets [an] 8 [or a] 9 [out of 10], and it's not because she necessarily brings a Bible to class, but that the organic experiences of her faith coming up happened most often in her class. And then they were spoken about after they happened.

Conversely, for this same student the two other professors she ranked were given 5 out of 10 because of the lack of organic expression: one was given a 5 because of a lack of "active trying" to have "faith moments," and the other would speak or do "truthful things" but then go "backwards and... apologizes, and when she apologizes she tries to bring up a Scripture or something... which we're not really looking for. And we tell her this, and I believe she understands that, she just gets self-conscious, like, 'Oh, I wasn't supposed to do that because this is a Christian school.'" Similar to S1, S3 also stated that one of the greatest influencers in her life verbalized her efforts at faith integration, in addition to letting her actions reinforce her faith. Thus the "integrity" component of organic IFL seems to suggest, if not necessarily require, that perceived meaningful IFL occurs when it is both lived out and spoken of by a modeler. The natural way in which this occurs, the "organic" component, keeps this verbalization from being contrived or forced upon the situation. It therefore implies that any person who models positive IFL must have a level of spiritual maturity that allows for honesty, care for others, and an ever-present awareness of the interaction between Christian faith and lived experience.

Within the alumni/ae interviews, integrous and organic modeling of faith integration was present in all five participants. A1 stated that one of her top-rated professors "walks with integrity." A2's top-rated professor "never missed an opportunity to, even if it completely derailed the class for an entire session, to talk about faith and faith living out in our lives and why that was so important." This was understood to be part of an organic expression of IFL, based on the heart of the professor and the attitude of the class on any given day. A3's ideal IFL in a classroom was based on actual classes he took, where faith integration was modeled organically. He states,

> A lot of it [faith integration] is by example. Like, live—actions speak louder than words, and live a life of example, people are going to notice. And the professors and things that I feel most did that are the ones who lived by example and didn't say, "Alright, here's the faith integration part, pick your favorite verse and how you can act it out." They just were. It wasn't a particular part, or week, or class, it just was. And that's when I'm feeling it's most effective, is when you're living by example and doing it.

Also, as with valuing, A3 gave an example of a professor whose approach to acting, which largely dealt with thinking about the other people on stage, mirrored her approach to teaching and to life: others came first. He was able to observe this because he encountered this particular professor (and another similar professor) in multiple settings: as a director and a professor, and in multiple school-related functions off campus. Thus, his particular view of this faculty member, and the faculty in general, tended toward a more "holistic" vantage point. Continuing on, one of A4's top-rated professors had strong convictions (though she was careful to point out that this professor was not abrasive) and was willing to "call out when things were weird or wrong." This demonstrated integrity between what the professor believed and how they interacted with the students around them. Finally, A5 gave an example of a director/professor who modeled "having faith as a priority" in his attitude and the atmosphere he created in the theater space, which illustrated integrity through how he approached his craft and the students.

The fifth type of modeling which students perceived from their faculty members was the modeling of *practices*, specifically the practices of *prayer* and *study*. It was unclear from the data whether the students and alumni/ae first valued these practices, and so consequently looked for them in their faculty, or if the faculty first practiced them and consequently they became important to the students. But in either case all four students referenced both of these practices and spoke of their influence, three of the five alumni/ae referenced prayer, and all five alumni/ae made mention of the modeled practice of study. S1, S2, S4, A1, A2, and A3 all spoke of both prayer and study as being parts of the ideal IFL, signifying that these practices held significant importance in their own spiritual development (A5 also mentioned the modeling of study as an ideal part of the IFL in a class and a production).

S1's references to modeled prayer and study both were found in how she talked about ideal IFL in a production setting: prayer was ideal when done communally with her cast and director, and study was ideally found in the dissection of a script, character studies, and writing exercises that pertained to the show. Both of these were modeled to her by her fellow castmates and director, and both were valuable enough that they were understood to be part of the ideal way faith integration happened in a theatrical setting.

S2 also spoke of study and prayer as ideals in IFL, though for her, study ideally happened in a classroom setting, and prayer in a production: for study, this included "pulling apart people and characters and shows" and finding the truthfulness in them; and for prayer, as for S1, this included group prayer by the directors, cast, and crew, which was understood to be very important because of the "heavy responsibility" of storytellers to tell their stories truthfully. Further, for S2 her second-highest ranked professor modeled study through the way they approached topics through the lens of their Christian faith. "They would take the time in their classes to just approach a topic that you didn't realize could be approached from such a faith standpoint and make it completely make sense and blow your mind."

S3's top-rated professor was one who modeled study through the way he approached the subject matter in his classes and productions. This professor would discuss the morality of characters and playwrights, and interweave conversation about how "intentional we should be about dealing with 'dark' or 'heavy' material, and how it can be unbelievably vulnerable and touching and revealing to human nature if done well, but can be very scarring and dangerous if not." Thus, for S3, the modeling of study was closely connected with the personal ramifications and purposes of the study, and the way she should approach her work. Further, this same professor prayed "a lot" for the class. In fact, all three of the professors she referred to prayed often. In an interesting comparison, however, S3's lowest-rated professor

> prayed for us... but the class felt very secular.... [It] didn't feel super faith centered. And I think with a lot of the material we were working with, it was hard to make it faith centered because we were dealing with some really like, heavy stuff. And for good reasons too, like, I really enjoyed that we got the heavy stuff out of the way right off the bat.... But that being said, I think that it could have been taken... a lot less lightly. Like [the professor] could have explained a little bit more.

Thus, for S3, prayer was important but it was important in the context of the larger spiritual awareness of the classroom instruction, and an intentional concern for the personal effect that embodied acting can have on a person, particularly a young Christian person of faith.

Finally, S4 also spoke about the importance of both modeled prayer and study. He said prayer was ideal to have both in the classroom and in production settings, and he gave an example of a professor who prayed for him personally during the run of a show. He also made several references to the practice of study, and said that it also was an ideal component of faith integration in the classroom, specifically in how being a Christian affects the way one approaches a role, and how being a Christian affects the way one should interact with cast and crew. "We'll sit and have discussions as a person of faith or as a Christian, 'how do you go about this situation?' if we're talking about a scene or whatnot, [or] if it's an acting class or it's a technical theatre class when you're kind of being placed in a hypothetical situation or a movie or if you're backstage and you're working with someone who is difficult." He also cited a professor who challenged him during a particular course and helped him learn how to study through the exploration of the acting experience and specific techniques, and that push in professional technique also connected with his faith. For him, unlike for the other students, he used the term "faith" to "describe humanity, really getting to understand the color spectrum of emotions." Thus, the work ethic and studious expectation of the professor allowed him to grow professionally and in how he understood his faith.

For the alumni/ae the examples and data given were much the same as they were for the students. A1 saw prayer as important enough to list it as an ideal for IFL in a production, specifically because it fosters unity and fellowship, and because it demonstrates care for her wellbeing (her top-rated professors did this as well). She also knew that professors were interested in her own spiritual growth through the way they communicated the connections between their own faith and their profession, thus illustrating the way they studied and applied their own work to their Christian beliefs, and at the same time providing a model to follow.

A2, like A1, also saw prayer as part of the ideal expression of IFL in a class, and saw it modeled in her mentor. Additionally, study was presented in the form of an ideal classroom assignment, where a student could "interview or shadow someone in their desired field who is living out a Christian worldview, and write a reflection paper on it." This shadowing illustrates one way that a student could examine how a professional prepares for (or studies for) a role, for directing a production, or for teaching a theatre class, and model their own study practices after what they observed. She also mentioned that discussions with professors "in and out of class" were very formative for her faith, as they illustrated the knowledge that these people had.

Continuing the trend, A3 saw prayer as part of the ideal expression of IFL, this time in a production setting. It was also listed as an example of IFL in a class that he had taken and in a production that he was a part of. Further, his top-rated professor prayed for students all the time. As for the practice of study, he understood that a professor's personal integration between what they learn and how they understand its relationship to faith was found in how they chose to teach their classes and what information they presented, and the ideal IFL in a classroom included this type of intentional approach to integrating faith and study.

Unlike most of their fellow alumni/ae and the current students, neither A4 nor A5 made any mention of prayer in their interviews. The modeling of study was present in two of A4's top-rated professors, however, both of which demonstrated critical thinking skills that integrated their Christian faith with their profession. Further, study was part of A5's ideal IFL in a classroom and in a production, where he saw the role of the professor as one who is "demonstrating action" and modeling what they know for others to learn through actions and explanation. He gave the example of one director who talked with a cast about the Biblical themes within a particular story, and how, by hearing how the director had studied and evaluated the text for its spiritual significance, it "helped me to see the show differently."

The last type of modeling that needs a very brief statement here is *peer modeling*. Even though the vast majority of references from the student and alumni/ae participants dealt with faculty as models, there were a few instances where peers were cited as being influential in this area. Some instances were very subtle, such as studying together as a class and hearing how other students approached a role or subject. One student, S1, made a point to state that her cohort of peers was influential in her faith. "We don't only see each other in class, we see each other outside of class. So that the relationships that we have inside of class are rooted in something, you know? I'm not just trusting you because you're an actress, I'm trusting you because last night we had this conversation and we have an understanding of one another." S2 thought that her peers were interested in her faith, but largely because, as a senior, she was now in a mentor or model role for younger students. "You can see it in the way that they watch you, in the way that they come to you with like, vulnerability, or fear, or all these other things. When they come to you for wisdom and answers." Thus her peer modeling was not connected to those whom she perceived as influential in her own life, but how she perceived herself as being a peer model to younger students.

A4 understood that her peers became models to her because of the way that both studying and valuing were modeled by their shared professors. Even though she disagreed with various stances taken by her fellow classmates, "because in class we were trained to discuss things a certain way, outside of class we discussed things a certain way. It can get really scary in other places I'm sure, but we gave each other room to disagree, to do what we needed to do."

A5 admitted he was greatly influenced by his peers. "Being surrounded by a group of artists with faith as a priority for what they did helped form in me... a focus of thinking the same way, if that makes sense, making faith a priority in what I do." Their influence as models who cared both about their spiritual journeys and their artistic endeavors "definitely influenced who I am and what I believe."

S3 had the most overt and lengthy reference to peer modeling. Though she thought peer modeling was less influential than either faculty or staff modeling, and though she was "not looking to them for an example," she spoke effulgently about a fellow student who was "Christ-like about the way that she approached being in the theatre department and being a friend and being a loved one." This fellow student was gracious in her relationships, was kind, acknowledged everyone, was attentive to direction, was engaged, and "put her all into everything she did." For S3, all of this was modeling Christ. She had a "realistic show of faith. Not fake, not plastic, and NOT by any means perfect. Just an honest-to-God attempt to reveal Christ through everyday life, actions, words."

These six types of modeling (*decision making, interpersonal, valuing, organic, practices,* and *peer*) all represent one of the largest, most influential components of how students and alumni/ae perceived effective faith integration in their program. With the addition of mentoring (both *intentional* and *in situ*), these two categories serve as the most overt ways that IFL was experienced by the student population (past and present) interviewed for this study. But they are not the only ways. Let us now turn our attention to the third cluster of meaning that arose from the interviews, *preparation.*

## Preparation

Over the course of the interview process it became clear that IFL was not only something witnessed but something *experienced.* Often times these experiences were intentional and were understood to be part of the learning process that occurs in an educational environment. Consequently, sometimes students undertook particular exercises that helped them not only grow in their craft but also in their faith. Other times the discovery process of theatrical learning led to breakthroughs that were unexpected and meaningful, but that nonetheless were achieved because of the challenging environment into which the students placed themselves or that the professors fostered in their classes or productions. In both cases, however, learning and growth occurred because students were *prepared* (or preparing) for learning and growth. This preparation took many forms, but two main areas came to the forefront in the interviews: prayer and study.

Three of the four students, and three of the five alumni/ae, mentioned the act of praying as an important aspect of the way they experience and understand IFL. While being prayed *for* was important in modeling faith integration, the *act* of praying by the students also seemed to have some influence. All six participants who referenced prayer in this way spoke of it as being part of the ideal way for IFL to occur, particularly when done with other people. In this instance, all three students spoke of prayer with their casts as being very important: S2, in her speaking about prayer, gave the example of a production that she was involved in that was "covered... in prayer... by its cast and by people surrounding it," and S4 said that prayer created a "shared space with a common goal," a goal that acknowledged the "One who gave us these gifts and passions." For S4 it also served to remove the distractions of life which often surrounded a production. Interestingly, even though the act of praying was often mentioned, it was usually done as part of a list. It appeared to be presented as an "obvious" answer, one that filled in the mental and spatial gap in the conversation while the student looked for a more concrete or profound answer. And no student stated or implied that private prayer held any value in how they understood faith integration in their chosen field.

For the alumni/ae, prayer also largely happened communally, with cast members or fellow classmates. A1 believed that it was important to come "together in prayer at the top of a production [to pray] for everyone that's a part of it. I know that Satan kind of likes to pick apart things that he sees are going to be good and that will bring that light into this world." She spoke of an example where prayer was used to foster unity and fellowship. "I know the times we did pray as a cast, it was very moving.... There was a unity that you can't really explain. Doing a show with anyone you get that sense of community, but I think praying together brings in that element of true fellowship with one another." Thus prayer served as a way to rebuff forces that may try to divide or inhibit the positive work of a theatrical production, and it fostered community. A2, in speaking about the ideal integration of faith and learning in a classroom, stated that she would follow her professors' example and pray for her students and encourage them to pray for each other. From her own experiences she knew that being prayed for was spiritually formative, and that the act of praying (in her case with a mentor) was important for her own maturation. A3, like A1, spoke highly of praying before rehearsals and performances with a cast as being an ideal way to integrate faith into a production setting. "It's just kind of like, showing that, look, we care about this production, we're going to pray over it, and it's important to us.... We're just, you know, going to pray God's blessing on

57

this production." He also listed examples of prayer in classes and in productions where it served to foster community and provided ways for instructors to "live by example."

Though prayer was often mentioned as a significant part of IFL, it was not nearly as prevalent in the conversation as the practice of study. This practice was mentioned by all four students and four of the five alumni/ae, but unlike prayer it manifested in several forms, depending on the direction of the interview conversation.

For S1, study appeared in several places. First, it was part of an example of IFL in a classroom, where she engaged in breathing the name of YHWH over and over again with her classmates in order to see how it affected her body and gave meaning to the word/Name. This activity was meditative in fashion and brought God's presence to the student, and the sharing of the experience with others in the class was profoundly powerful for her. This activity was understood to be part of her larger study of movement, but the process of studying influenced the way she integrated her faith with her learning. Study was also understood to be part of the ideal IFL in a production setting, where the cast would seek to connect the script (characters and story) with Christian faith. Finally, S1 gave several examples of IFL in both the classroom and production settings where study occurred and was deemed relevant to faith integration. These included examining stories of death and resurrection in writing exercises, developing character studies in order to create empathy and respect for others, and comparing characters and/or elements of a story within a play to Biblical characters and/or stories to illustrate Christian principles or theology.

For S2 there were also several instances throughout the interview where study came up, though the majority of the examples dealt with study as self-discovery. Examples included "pulling apart people and characters and shows" in order to better understand the "truth" of them, learning about humanity through research around a production or a class, and engaging in conversations about cross-cultural and interreligious identities of certain characters within a show. She stated very clearly that any professor who cared about integrating faith and learning would never force their own ideas on a student, but would rather let them discover and learn for themselves.

> I feel like any professor who is truthfully bringing faith integration into learning is going to present you with their truth and with their struggles, but ultimately they lay it out for you in order to find it for yourself. They don't tell you which way is right, which way is wrong. They may try to guide you in some ways, but ultimately they allow you to explore that as they lay it out for you.

Because of this perspective, study becomes a way in which students, particularly S2, could weigh the examples and presentations of the professors with their own knowledge learned so far. Consequently, upon reflecting back on the changes in her life since she started her undergraduate career, S2 stated that her theatrical experience had a profound impact on her spiritual growth, in no small part because of the self-discovery study process. She discovered that in stories, "these people are messy and life is messy because it's a journey, and how, if life is a story there is no point to a story that stays the same. A story is beautiful because it has these ups and downs, and these redemptions, and these mess ups and failures. And faith is the same way." Through the study of storytelling she learned that having all the answers (or thinking she had all the answers to life) was not only impossible but self-destructive. Instead, because of studying theatre through the lens of faith, she discovered that admitting weakness and lack of full knowledge leads to a "freedom that allows God to dwell there because that's his place." For her, failure leads to growth. Though long, the quote below captures the essence of what she learned.

> [T]hrough dealing with stories, and figuring that out, and just realizing that life is a beautiful broken journey... I found myself as of this year, through all the four years, thanking God for sin, which sounds very strange! But I noticed that, you know, without our failures, without sin, we wouldn't get to experience this wonderful, wonderful gift that is grace. Which is so core to who God is. And so often we get so upset about the struggles and all the horrible things you've gone through and the ways I've messed up and "why did I have to experience this, or this, or this?" But all those things allow us to illuminate who God is in his beauty. And it's these paradoxes that I think I've finally been able to kinda wrap my mind around, that Scripture's filled with paradox, which to me seemed like contradiction to start with coming in here... But realizing that these paradoxes exist because without them, without joy, or without pain you wouldn't be able to experience joy, and without hurt you wouldn't be able to experience healing and hope. Which is such a painful thing to come to terms with, but when you do it's really quite beautiful, I think. And to be able to go through all of those things, and with characters, and in my own life, and with friends, I started to realize, you know, praise God for the struggle, praise God for all of the shit. Because that's what has allowed me to really truly understand God's character, and without it I wouldn't know who He is as well as I do now.

Though this quote no doubt encompasses the near totality of her collegiate life, it is telling that she places "characters" from her studies on par with lived experiences with respect to their influence on her spiritual growth and maturation. The embodiment of characters, and/or the study and development around them, provided a powerful resource whereby she was able to better understand what she believed, and gave her a greater sense of God's character. Further, these characters, when placed in the stories in which they reside, helped her to discover the beauty in an imperfect human life and gave her the freedom to accept failure as growth in her own life.

If S2 spoke at length about study as self-discovery, S3 barely touched on it at all. For her, study was something that was designed to provide tools to be used in future work. In her answer to the ideal way to integrate faith and learning in a classroom she mentioned the inclusion of specific faith integration assignments, such as papers, projects, and presentations, which was different than many of her fellow students. The purpose of the assignments was that they were "established routine things that are specifically meant or designed to take Biblical theories or Biblical mindsets and integrate them into the course that you're doing," so that one may retain one's faith in secular environments and show Christ to others in applicable ways. Nearly all of her references to study fell under *modeling*: how did the professor study, or how did they approach faith integration? For her, this was far more important for her own spiritual growth than her own practice of study.

Finally, S4 understood the value of study to be in the way it enhanced his own ability as an actor. Since he understood faith to be the recognition of one's own humanity, specifically "realizing that you're not God," study provided a way to think deeply about self and about characters, to "study human beings on an emotional, intellectual, and spiritual level" and address their moral and spiritual dimensions. In a class that ideally integrates faith and learning, S4 said he would look for discussions of the relationship between Christian faith and approaches to roles and interactions with others. Study also meant finding ways to remove the distractions of life from interfering in a performance, such as through prayer. Further, the practice of study, particularly related to character study and acting techniques, gave him great faith in himself and his own abilities, "knowing that I could do it." His top-rated professor helped him to understand his "humanity," which referred to working through emotions and making him stronger and humbler as a person, and his second-highest rated professor helped him explore his "vulnerability" in his acting approach. Thus it appears that for S1, study was about finding how theatre fit into her Christian worldview; S2 saw it as a means to discover more about what she actually believed; S3 valued it as a way to retain vestiges of faith in a largely secular environment (and as largely an intellectual exercise at a predominantly Christian program); and S4 understood it to be a tool to enhance his approach to the acting craft.

Within the alumni/ae interviews, study appeared in much the same fashion as it did in the student interviews. For A1, study was largely about self-discovery. When asked for examples of the ideal way to integrate faith into a class, she mentioned hypothetical assignments that were student-research driven and that were geared toward learning more about oneself. "I believe that the Lord has given us each gifts in ways He wants us to bring His light to the world. And so I definitely think that it's helping the students to find what that gift is, and use it to bring light into the darkness [of the industry]." For her, "more hands-on experience was beneficial to me as a student," and therefore study was understood to be projects and assignments that allowed her to practice or examine her craft while learning through experience how to integrate her faith with her work.

If study was experiential for A1, then it was largely an intellectual exercise for A2. The practice of study for her was part of "structured discussions." Though some examples were given that were more action-oriented (such as interviewing or shadowing a person working in the entertainment industry), these assignments still were done in order to "help [students] begin to formulate their thoughts" about their faith and Christian worldview. One example of a "structured discussion" was a conversation in a class that "discussed the pros and cons of Method acting. This led to discussions about Christ's incarnation, and how our hope in Him is essential to maintain a healthy acting psyche." This idea of a healthy "psyche," which came about through the practice of study (in this case communal conversation), greatly assisted A2 in her professional life after graduation. "In the midst of playing a drug addict [in a production], I can hold on to the hope I have in Christ while still playing a character who may have lost all her hope, so that when the experience is over for me, I can let go of those emotions and they do not become part of me." Thus study, though intellectual in practice, had very practical applications and purposes for this alumna.

In a similar vein to A1's experience, A4's understanding of study largely dealt with discovery. However, though it included elements of *self*-discovery, for her it was largely about the discovery of how other people understood the relationship between faith and art or faith and the world. An example of IFL in an ideal classroom included examining "different people of different kinds of faith and their journey in their art." Another example from a real class was an assignment where she was asked to find a current story in the news and bring "that story to life and [talk] about what that meant... [and] not just [be] so introspective and what are my issues, but what's going on out here and how can I make an impact." These exercises were undertaken in order to better understand other people, and to discover how her skills in theatre could improve the lives of others. Finally, for A5, study involved finding the "meaning or moral that you can take out of [a show] that's worthwhile and worth telling." Thus, similar to the student responses, it appears that for A1, study was a means to discover more about what she actually believed; A2 saw it as an intellectual pursuit that prepared her to spiritually and emotionally handle the challenges of her career; A4 valued it as a way to learn about other people; and A5 understood it a way to enhance his spiritual perspective of a production.

*Motivation*

The fourth and last of the large clusters of meaning that came to light from the interviews was *motivation*. That is, why did all nine current and former students believe that faith integration was important enough for their own spiritual growth that they chose to study at a faith-based institution?[10] And what motivated them all to say that faith integration was important and beneficial for working in theatre?

---

[10] It is important to note that three of the four students (S1, S2, and S3) chose this particular University first because it was a Christian university, as did all five of the alumni/ae. While all four students were theatre majors and knew that they wanted to study theatre, only one chose the school solely because of the degree program; the remaining three wanted to attend a Christian university, then find one with a quality theatre program. The same was true for all five alumni/ae. For S4, the draw was the "friendly" and "tight-knit community" within the department; S1 just wanted to study theatre; S2 wanted a program "that had a strong faith underbelly to it... a good Christian grounding.... So I came here and I found a faith community... that was based in love and had so much freedom and joy in faith rather than these overbearing, legalistic rules and standards"; and S3 was drawn away from another school to this university because it was Christian, had a theatre major, has passionate and enthusiastic students and faculty, was professional in its approach, and sought to integrate faith with practice, in that order. Two alumni/ae stated that there was a connection between choosing this particular Christian university and the university's theatre department, which was described as "where I was supposed to be" (A1), and a place where "I [could]... be challenged... [and] sit next to someone who has a completely different worldview than me." The remaining three alumni/ ae picked the university first because it was a "faith-based" (A2) school "where God wanted me to go" (A3), and then later chose to major in theatre. Among the six faculty participants in the study there was an even split: three chose to teach at the university because of its particular mission statement and faith-based environment, while the other three chose it because of the theatre program and the particular students who were involved in it.

Like with modeling and preparation, no single answer encompasses all of the reasons given. Among the student participants, S2, for example, implied that faith integration motivated her to better *serve* the audience and the story through truthful telling and portrayal of a character. S4 acknowledged that there was motivation to grow professionally but also to *worship* through prayer and acknowledge the "One who gave us these gifts and passions." And both S2 and S4 were motivated by being challenged, both professionally and in their spiritual growth: S2's top-rated professor challenged her "to go further than you've ever gone, and to try harder than you've tried before," and S4's top-rated professor challenged him to give more than he thought possible, which was "such a strong spiritual experience because… we're meant to feel in color." But all four students said that their top motivation for faith integration was that it gave their work *purpose* For S1 faith is "completely intertwined with theatre," and therefore it gives value to the stories that she tells and helps her understand them better. It also provides motivation to keep working in theatre.

> You need to understand what you're doing… and why it's so important
> to you. And so, for me, having it deeply rooted and related to my faith
> gives it all the value necessary. And it keeps me in it, because acting is
> really hard on many levels, and so it's easy to want to give up.

S2 understood the purpose of pursuing a career in theatre as following in Jesus's footsteps as a storyteller. "Here we're getting majors to be storytellers, and Jesus was the very first storyteller of all time and probably one of the most profound and gifted at it. So in some ways I consider it a very heavy calling on our lives. If you're going into that sort of a thing you're following in the footsteps of Jesus, so it has that sort of power." As a storyteller, S2 understood her purpose as telling the truth, specifically what she referred to as "capital-T Truths," which are God's Truths that "exist in everyday life, in every life that is out there. They just are universal." These Truths, which include things like "pain" and "hurt," must be told truthfully in order that an audience may "evidently see God's hand and things pointing to God and pointing to faith and grace." Thus the purpose of truthful storytelling is that it might lead to people discovering God's presence within the activities of life. Like S2, S3 also understood the purpose of theatre as bringing "light to God" and God's creation, what she refers to as the "right reasons" of theatre, though she did not elaborate on how this was done. In large part it seemed to reflect more on her own understanding and spiritual growth, but with the supposed implication that that growth in knowledge would lead to sharing and a kind of theatrical evangelism.

Finally, S4 understood the purpose of faith integration as a means to help him "learn how to love and accept people in general" because it, combined with theatrical study and experiences, exposed him to different types of people. "It really humbles you, makes you realize that you're no better than any other person and that everyone is capable of being loved no matter what." Interestingly, he differentiated his own understanding of the purpose of IFL from those of his professors. From his understanding, they engaged with IFL because they wanted to "send out people of faith into this industry… that's part of their… mission and it's part of what they want to apply in the classroom." Thus, from his perspective, while their purposes ended when a student graduated, he understood the purpose of faith integration as recognizing the "humanity" of self and others in order that they might be loved and accepted.

Among the alumni/ae participants the reasons given for their motivation were also just as varied, though they tended to be more consistent. A1, A2, and A4 made mention of the value of corporate guidance or *teamwork*: since theatre can never be done alone, working with others reinforced the "things Christ said" and did for all people and provided opportunities to "love your neighbor" (A2). Also, having opportunities to work toward a common theme or goal (A4) and to be a Christ-like example to others on a team (A1) were factors that motivated spiritual growth as well. For A1 specifically, to have friends and family affirm her talents in theatre, and that these talents came from God, was deemed an important part of her overall spiritual growth and maturity during her time as a student, and this corporate affirmation motivated her to continue working in the field.

Further, A2 and A4 all spoke about being motivated through being *challenged*, both professionally and spiritually, by the faculty and peers. While discussing formative experiences with her peers, A2 said, "We would struggle with our faith together and pray together and even, my freshman year one of my friends started a prayer group.... Yeah, so I think being there for each other was really important to us." This "struggle" of faith was understood by her to be very important in her spiritual development, and part of what motivated her to continue. A4 made a negative correlation between spiritual care and being challenged: when asked to answer the question, "A professor who cares about my spiritual growth would never...?" she responded, "Would never not challenge me.... Someone who had invested in my spiritual growth and knew the kind of growth that I was going through, they'd be able to recognize when I was not doing well, or not pushing myself, so they would never not challenge me if they could see my going the opposite direction or backtracking." She also gave an example of when she turned in an assignment done "very flippant[ly]" and the professor called her out. Thus, for her, a professor who cares for her, both spiritually and professionally, would push her to do better, and indeed, this very thing was mentioned again when she spoke about two of her top-rated professors.

The two types of motivation that seemed to have the greatest resonance with the alumni/ae, however, were *service* and *purpose*. Four of the five alumni/ae referred to their theatrical work as service. A1 saw her time on stage as a way to "perform for the Lord." This also was connected with the purpose that she found in acting. She stated,

> We all want [applause], and we all need that too, but I think it... should be instilled in the actors that, you are enough, you go out there and use your gifts to the fullest, and perform for the Lord who gave you those gifts. And I think, at least for me that kind of would change my perspective on things. The applause would still be nice, and it would feel so good opening up the show finally and getting a laugh or two, but I think at the end of the day it would just kind of bring [us] back to a place of realizing what's truly important.... Because then you can go forward into productions outside of a Christian environment where that's already instilled in you and you're not starving for that response, because I'm

doing my best, this is for the Lord, this isn't for you, you, you, and you.
This is just for Him. And I truly think that's one of the greatest things that
we can teach students. Especially in this industry because it gets crazy
out there.

For her, her service was performing for God, and this service gave purpose
to what she was doing, which was "bringing truth and life to a story" as
Christ "brought truth and life into our story here on earth and gave us a
purpose."

A2 spoke in some detail about a production that she was a part of where
the cast was, as she termed it, a

service team. We would go and try and serve the place that we were going
to [perform at], and have good attitudes and serve one another... and
treat everyone we met with love and respect. And just try to be a good
example wherever we went so that our message was, hopefully, well
received.

This idea of using theatre as a way to serve others, both within and outside of the
production, was very important for her. And as with A1, she connected this concept
with her understanding of theatre's purpose and her own, which was "using the gifts
and talents that [God has] blessed me with to spread the gospel and spread His love
to as many people as possible." The purpose, then, of faith integration within theatre
is that it "helps remind us that there is more to life than just this one audition, and
more to life than trying to find jobs.... It teaches us to place our value in Christ, and
it teaches to view our life as a calling."

Unlike the others, A3 made no mention of service in his interview, but he
did describe faith integration as providing a "consistent and reliable" place to stand
as an actor.

It's beneficial because it helps you know who you are, and there's a
danger when you're an actor, that you get caught up in trying to be
someone else, or chase something else, or be what someone else wants
you to be, and faith is the thing that can be consistent and reliable.

He was motivated to integrate his faith with his craft because it provided a reference
point for who he really was: a person with a "relationship with Jesus Christ."

Similarly to A1, A4 saw theatrical practice as a service, a way to continue
the work of Jesus, who was a "storyteller," and to let the Holy Spirit "get very deep
into the hearts of people's souls, bring out the ugliest things and the most beautiful
things" in life in order that others might experience God. This service also gave her
work purpose, and helped her deal with industry rejection and find a "home base"
for dealing with the difficult emotions and ugliness of embodied character work.

And lastly, A5 was motivated by "stewardship," or service to the rightful
owner of something. In this context it referred to the understanding that just as the
physical resources of a theatre are not his property, neither are the gifts and talents
that theatre artists have their own. As he states, we are to be "using the gifts that we
have, have been given, have been loaned to us... to create something meaningful
and worthwhile that is pleasing to God." This desire to "please" God gives his work
purpose and meaning, and helps him to "actively apply the teachings of Jesus to
[my] day to day life and actions."

*Connectivity*

The last cluster of meaning that illustrates the way students and alumni/ae were influenced in their spiritual growth and in how they perceived faith integration is what this researcher calls *connectivity*. Connectivity refers to the relationships formed with faculty, staff, and peers, and to the way theatrical training and exercise connected the students with humanity as a whole. Connectivity appeared in all nine student and alumni/ae interviews, making it an essential part of understanding how past and present students perceived their own growth and the efforts of faith integration in their department.

In one part of her interview, S1 spoke of how she had changed "tremendously" during her time at the university. This change was manifest in how she was able to better connect with the human" in story and in life. Biblical and theological knowledge is

> absolutely important but if you can't just connect with the soul of a person
> that means nothing. It's like in Ecclesiastes... everything is meaningless,
> and everything is meaningless without God. So all your knowledge of the
> Bible is meaningless if you still cannot connect with the human being.

This connection, fostered through her theatrical training, led to empathy for others, which allowed her to care more for the person instead of only focusing on what they did or did not do. As she says, she learned how to "judge... with love." As if picking up on the same empathetic theme, A4 found connectivity with an audience member:

> I was in the middle of [two] show[s] at that time and I was so tired, and
> I was like, "I want to get the show over with, I want to get back home, I
> have to do homework, I have so much to do right now" and so... it was
> one of those shows [where I was] going through the motions.... And this
> woman came up to me afterwards and she was crying and so emotional.
> And she gave me this big old hug and said, "What you said in that last
> line about a boyfriend being just there," she said "my daughter just said
> that about the relationship that she was in."... [W]atching the story and
> watching my character made it kind of click for her and so she kind of
> understood where her daughter was at at that point. So we talked about
> her daughter and we prayed together, and for me, number one I realized
> how selfish I was being..., and [number two], also proving the point that
> God's work will get done whether my heart is in it or not.

The unexpected connectivity that she found with an audience member, even when she wasn't looking for it or intending it, refocused her attention on her purpose as a performer.

For S2, connectivity fostered respect for others as well, but whereas S1 spoke more in the abstract, S2 spoke directly about her peers. Fellow students helped her grow in knowledge and critical thinking, both with respect to theatre and to her faith.

> I can probably list off like five or ten people who have had a substantial
> impact [on my spiritual growth]. When you're going through these
> classes with people who are also experiencing the prophetic wisdom of
> [X] or [X] or all these people, being able to go and live life with them
> outside of class, being able to ruminate in these ideas and just, things that
> can tend to rack your mind and brain, is sometimes the biggest help.
> Because you can be there in that classroom, in that moment, for 15
> minutes where you feel like your mind just exploded, your world just

blew up.... But what really matters is being able to go out from there, as that sits in your mind and marinates..., and to bring up those questions, and to sit and have these long conversations of frustration and panic and joy and who knows what else, as you both kind of sit there and try to figure out what that means for you personally, and how is that going to shift your life or convict you or reassess how you do things.

The importance of community and connectedness for S2 lay in how it provided a safe place for the dissemination of knowledge and the implications and applications of that knowledge for the Christian theatre practitioner. In a similar (but shorter) fashion, A5 also referred to the connectivity of the theatre environment as being formative for his faith. "Just being surrounded by a group of artists with faith as a priority" made faith a priority for him too.

Out of all of the students, S3 gave the most cursory of nods to connectivity, but even still it was understood to be an important part of her spiritual journey. In the same way that she understood the purpose of theatre as bringing "light to God" and God's creation, so too community and connectivity with others allowed S3 to "bring light to God and reveal things about humanity" to others. "Theatre connects people on such a different level than any other art form, and there is something to be said about the fellowship and community that connection creates." Most of the examples that were given of this connection/community were from those whom she admired as role models, such as a peer who was very influential because of how she treated others, and several professors who were caring, "compassionate," "respectful," "attentive," "understanding," and who fostered a "healthy working environment." Though these more directly fall under the *modeling* cluster, they also illustrate the importance of the connection between S3 and those whom she viewed as important for her education and her spiritual health. This same type of connectivity was also present in A1, who spoke at length about professors who modeled "Christian leadership" through their care, compassion, and work ethic, and it was also present in A2, who gave several examples of professors and peers who were "formative" because of the connections she forged with them during her time as a student (e.g., one was an intentional mentor, and several were fellow classmates or roommates).

S4 spoke of connectivity as being part of his ideal IFL. For him, shared growth and vulnerability through the mounting of a production or in a class creates a "spiritual bond" between the participants. This bond creates a supportive environment where all are included and no one is better than another. Citing an instance of praying together as a cast, he stated,

I feel really connected to everyone in those moments, and we're all recognizing one thing all together. It's that moment [when]... we're all showing support for one another and realizing what our common goal is,... where you get to take your ego and shove it to the side for a minute. And you realize that the whole situation, the whole production... is much bigger than how much stage time you have.

The supportive nature of community came up again later in the interview. When asked about the influence of peers in particular on his spiritual growth, S4 replied that peers had the greatest influence, even more than faculty. When asked why he said,

We're all growing together, and these are the people we're working with, these are the people we will potentially work with once we leave here. And... going through struggles together, and you know, maybe not getting along at times and whatnot, it has a really big impact I think on how you view people because these are the people that—this is your generation specifically that you're growing with. And they're helping you see the world, or helping you realize how you see the world.

The connectivity of shared experiences, whether on stage, in the classroom, or in other collegiate locales, clearly played a part in how he understood his own spiritual growth. These connections had purpose not only for the years while he was a student but also for the future when he would move out into the professional world, and it was acknowledged that without these peers he would not have developed in his faith or his craft to the same extent that he did. Similarly, A3 also spoke of connectivity in his ideal IFL, stating that faith integration allows for a greater sense of community because it helps a person better know themselves and those around them. He grew in his faith largely because of the students in his class. "I even think that faith integration comes from time spent together.... Community is super important, and [this university] does community really well." Later he stated, "I had a very special class. The group of people who went through this program with me, I think is very unique." And, "[Spiritual growth] is about who's around you, and who's influencing you. So I don't think it had anything to do with being a theatre major or not being a theatre major, it's about who is there." Those whom he listed as "there" for him included a particularly influential peer, several faculty, and even a janitor.

*Negative IFL*

The last section of data that was an important part of the interview material is not so much a cluster of meaning as it is a cluster of significance. Two of the questions posed to participants asked what a professor who integrates faith and learning (or who cares for a student's spiritual growth) would *not* do. The purpose of these questions was to determine what students, alumni/ae, and faculty perceived as having a negative effect on a student's spiritual growth or understanding of their faith. The answers, by and large, were in line with the positive attributes mentioned by the participants: if a student said that being open-minded or caring was an important part of instruction, then being closed-minded or judgmental were listed as negative factors in their development. The actual breakdown of answers is as follows:

For S1, any professor who stifles a student's opinion or is closedminded in a way that prevents another from exploring Biblical interpretation hurts their efforts at faith integration. As she states, "If you don't allow other people to explore [Scripture] for themselves, and to let them get it into their own body and to live it, then you're forcing people just to be puppets. And puppets, after a while, don't like to have their strings pulled." Disagreement is acceptable, but it should be amicable. Further, a professor who cares about students' spiritual growth would never intentionally cause a student to lose hope, and would have a genuine faith that expresses itself naturally. She acknowledges that a professor can accidently cause a student to falter or lose faith, but intentionally killing the hope that a student has in

God would be near unpardonable. Additionally, doing one thing yet saying another, even if done with good intention, calls into question the character of the professor and makes them less impactful in their efforts to demonstrate or teach IFL. One professor was rated with a 5 out of 10 because she would do "things that Christians don't do," which was okay and even "helpful" at times, but then "she tries to apologize for it and to give us Christian responses which we're not really looking for." This disingenuous response actually detracted from what the professor was trying to correct and was perceived as a negative influence.

For S2, negative IFL was understood to occur when a professor would attempt to "force an idea upon you, or force you to pick one way or another." This was contrasted with professors who were truthful and honest with their own struggles and let students determine for themselves what to do with that information. Further, professors who cared about her spiritual growth "would never judge me.... They meet you where you are, and in that help you discover who God is in that place." This lack of judgment comes from a perceived position of spiritual depth and maturity on the part of the professor. Indeed, a professor who was thought to be "one-dimensional" in their expression of their faith (largely through their efforts at faith integration) was rated lower by S2 than professors that had a more organic and fluid approach.

For S3, a professor who successfully integrated faith and learning would never "take lightly or disregard what faith can be integrated into what we're doing." For her, meaningful faith integration started with the attitude and behavior of the professor. "If they do not treat it with respect and care, the students most likely will not either." In fact, on a scale of influence between 1 and 10, with 10 being the most influential factor in faith integration, she gave professorial attitude an 8. Along those same lines, S3 also said that any professor who cares about the spiritual growth of their students would never attempt to "separate theatre and Christianity." This is because of the discernment process needed by an actor in determining how to play a role, or *if* to play a role, specifically because of the influence of (potential) embodied sin on the actor's psyche and soul, and because of the desire for "something good to be taken from a character or a production."

For S4, a negative influence on faith and learning is the assumption that he does not need to grow in his faith, or that his faith is at the same point as that of other students. Because of the self-acknowledgment that his faith is still maturing, judgment placed upon him by a professor would inhibit this maturation process. "If they truly cared then I think it's important to not jump to judging [a person] when there's a mistake made, or when something new is learned about them." This theme of nonjudgment came up several times in the interview, and was deemed to be an important factor in how he understood his faith and the faith of others.

For A1, any professor who would "disrespect their students" was immediately at a disadvantage in achieving effective IFL. This disrespect would come in the form of a student being "torn down" and having numerous "negative thing[s]" brought up over and over again, specifically related to how a student learns. A nurturing and encouraging professor was understood to be the opposite of a disrespecting professor. A1 also said a professor who cared about a student's spiritual growth would never abuse the trust they have with students by exposing confidential material or by living a lifestyle that contradicts what they teach.

For A2, a professor who integrates faith and learning would never "dismiss or belittle a student's question or concern about... how their faith tied into their field... or life." For her, simply receiving acknowledgement about the value of a question was more important and impactful on her faith than getting an answer to the question. It provided validity to her concern, and consequently to her as a person. Further, she also stated that a professor who cared about her spiritual growth would never "tear down my faith" without building it back up. Since academic approaches to theological issues have a tendency to "deconstruct" what a student held to as true, leaving a student in that place of uncertainty and faithlessness was understood to be harmful. She felt that discussions of faith academic and could be useful in helping students identify what they do believe, even amidst the deconstruction, and that a caring professor would create space for that.

For A3, a professor who cared about integrating faith and learning would naturally do it because it was essential to their understanding of self. Citing a few examples, he stated that faith "is a part of who they are.... It's just like the way they lived and the way they handled themselves." Consequently, they could not *not* integrate faith into their teaching. Similarly, a professor who cared about spiritual growth in their students would "always care" because it is a part of their nature.

For A4, a negative example of IFL would be when a professor might shut down dialogue instead of "challenging" or "pushing" students to work through an issue. To the credit of her faculty, she could not give an example of a theatre department instructor who did this. Good professors "created an atmosphere where, no matter what was put out there, we could just sit on it and discuss it." This answer was given for both questions, and in both cases a professor who "challenged" her was understood to care about her spiritual growth and demonstrate effective IFL.

For A5, a professor who effectively integrated faith and learning would never "be unaccepting of an individual's [faith] journey, [or] condemn someone for not having it all right.... [They] would never put someone down for not being at their level." This answer was given for both questions.

All of these clusters of meaning, along with the cluster of significance for student and alumni/ae perceptions of negative IFL, constitute the data as it was presented during the interview and follow-up processes. From mentoring and modeling to motivation, preparation, and connectivity these answers completely summarize how the participants perceived and imagined faith integration happening within the theatre department during their undergraduate studies. But how does it compare with faculty perceptions and imaginings? With this data in mind, let us now turn our attention to what they had to say.

# Research Findings
## Faculty

**Actual Findings: Faculty**

If the students and alumni/ae had several points of variance among their answers, then the faculty had even more so. For this study, six current faculty members were interviewed, five of whom teach in the theatre department and one who taught several theatre courses and directed numerous productions but who now teaches in a related but different department. They will be identified here as F1, F2, F3, F4, F5, and F6. All six are full-time faculty and have countless interactions with the undergraduate student population on a daily basis. In order to preserve promised anonymity, and because it is easier to determine "who said what" among a stable yet small faculty pool whose makeup is public record, no demographic data for these six will be given and all faculty members will be referred to in the feminine. This is particularly important because several faculty members expressed concern regarding their answers to certain questions due to fear of how they might be perceived by the university administration in terms of its efforts to assess faculty faith integration. Whether the attention was real or imagined, certain faculty within the theatre department felt as if they were being scrutinized or that their work was being misunderstood by those who were doing the assessment, which is part of the faculty evaluation (and promotion) process at this university. This will come up as we move further into the faculty perceptions and ideals regarding faith integration. For these reasons the author has chosen to remove all possible identifying factors in order to maintain the trust that has been established with the faculty members.

Faculty responses to questions regarding faith integration were diverse and thoughtful. This was not surprising, given that all of them saw their work as part of a student's faith journey, and since every faculty member understood their own faith as playing an integral role in how they both taught their subject and approached their craft (both as an instructor and as a professional). Because of the diversity in answers, determining appropriate clusters of meaning proved a greater challenge than it did for the student and alumni/ae populations. However, through the coding process there eventually emerged six clusters that captured the essence of their responses and their understanding of effective IFL in their teaching and in the department. In no particular order, these clusters were *instruction, modeling, identity, mentoring, preparation,* and *motivation*.

*Instruction*

It should surprise no one that all six faculty members understood their instruction as an essential part of the IFL process. Over the course of the interviews, multiple pedagogical approaches were mentioned, from traditional lectures to student self-discovery. All were thought to have some role in effective IFL, but some were more universally mentioned by the faculty than others.

The two most-referenced types of instruction were what this author terms *engaged* instruction and *self-discovery*. The first, engaged instruction, refers to instruction that is designed to be student driven. Examples given included having students analyze art to see the messages in it (F1); an exercise where students examine a poem by a philosopher about playing ball with an eternal partner, and then physically play with a ball by themselves and then with each other to illustrate the poem (F2); improvisation exercises (F3); having students defend a play that was being produced at the university, or that the student would like to see done at the university (F4); exposing students to playwrights with radically different worldviews so that they could "shed light on our condition as humans created in the image of God" (F5); and having students observe another person and then perform a short, self-written piece about that person in order to discuss whether the exercise was faith-based (F6). These examples illustrate an engaged pedagogy that allows the student to actively participate in the learning process (physically, emotionally, cognitively, and/or spiritually). This type of engagement is believed by the faculty to then facilitate faith integration in some fashion. For example, F3, when speaking about improvisation, said,

> The book we're reading [in class], written by an unbeliever, or a non-Christian, is saying there's something about a certain moment of connection that is supernatural. I mean, they'll even say that these patterns exist, and we connect, and we do that amongst ourselves and then we do that for the audience. It's quite thrilling and it's quite something outside ourselves that begins to happen in the group, and by surrendering to one another, to one another's ideas.

F6, when recalling what she said to a group of actors, said that they "have to bring events from your own life and that you have experienced, whether they were painful or not, and marry them with that character so that when you utter those words you are sharing a part of yourself. That's a walking testimony." Thus, when students are instructed to give a part of themselves to the learning process and engage with it in ways that are beyond mere cognitive assent or dissent, then faith integration can occur because "God is at work in their work. Because God works through means. Through us, even us" (F3).

In addition to engaged instruction every professor also referenced self-discovery instruction. This type of instruction, named by the author, is instruction that is oriented in such a way that it allows the students to discover something new about themselves. In the case of this study it refers to how a faculty member thinks a particular form of instruction will provide space for a student's discovery of God, spirituality, or faith-driven morality to occur. Though closely affiliated with engaged instruction/learning, self-discovery is not necessarily predicated on the physical or emotional involvement of the student; it could occur through more traditional means of instruction, such as lectures. For example, F5 spoke about an instance where her students discovered (or confirmed) that their Christian worldview will be different than the prevailing worldview of the entertainment industry. This awareness, in the way that it was brought up in the context of that particular class, forced them to examine what they believe and why, so that it could be explained to future coworkers and colleagues.

Generally speaking, however, most of the self-discovery instruction mentioned by the faculty was a form of engaged learning. F1 referred to a show that was designed to let the audience decide the fate of the lead character based on the moral choices that he had made, thus prompting both the audience and the cast to examine how the character behaved and what was an appropriate fate, and how they themselves might be (or should be) judged based on their own choices and actions in life (it was intentionally designed to be self-reflective). F2 gave the example of an activity that highlighted "the holiness of breath," where students, as part of a warm-up exercise, were to breathe in and out the name of YHWH, providing a space for them to meditate on the name and discover the meaning of the name as it passed through their lips. F3 stated that improvisation can lead to self-discovery and one's relationship with those around him or her, as it requires a surrendering of self to the other person(s) and their ideas. F4 believed that students discover more about themselves through the roles they play, roles that may be uncomfortable or with which they have some uncertainty: "I think in a production there's a vulnerability that's... always there when you're asking students to get up on stage." This vulnerability allows them to examine their own fears, doubts, beliefs, and views of the world. And F6, referring to the same assignment listed above, stated that it was designed to make students think consciously about God existing outside of the Church, and how He uses them as artists. She states that faith integration is never "on the nose.... It's taking the organic, authentic moment that's really happening and having the students examine [it to see]... is Christ in that moment?" It's looking for a "transformational moment" where change happens in the actor, the cast, the audience, or any combination of these. Since all six of the faculty made references to some type of student self-discovery as part of their instruction, it, like engaged instruction, was understood to be important for effective IFL to take place.

As both engaged and self-discovery instruction were largely participatory, so too were the other forms of instruction given throughout the interviews. In fact, only two professors even mentioned or gave examples of lecture-style pedagogies: F1 spoke of lessons where she gave examples from her own life that were more lecture-based, and F2 said she would bring in quotes from philosophers and theologians to "show [faith's] relationship to the subject matter" of the class. It is not the opinion of the author that the other professors did not use lecture-style pedagogies in their classroom. To the contrary, there was some implied evidence from the interviews that at least five of the six used it often. But there seemed to be the understanding that this particular technique was not conducive to effective IFL in a theatrical context, at least in comparison to other, more engaging techniques. In addition to those listed above, other referenced pedagogies included *discussion* (four of the six professors mentioned this as important for effective IFL), *encouragement of students* (three of six), *organic IFL moments* (five of six), and paradoxically, *structured* instruction (three of six). Let us spend a few moments addressing these pedagogies.

Discussion-oriented instruction was understood to be an engaged style of learning where both students and faculty conversed together about a particular topic of interest. F1 intentionally sought out ways to foster this style of instruction, such as finding plays that addressed faith-based themes (e.g., sin nature, sacrifice, or the emptiness of life) because they could lead to "deeper discussions." She also did this through discussions about the Christian worldview and its relationship or comparison to other worldviews from other faiths and non-faiths. F4 sought out discussion both with students *and with fellow faculty* by offering resources related to faith integration within the arts. Indeed, for her, discussion was part of the ideal way for the integration of faith and learning to occur, and it was best when the students prompted the conversation. "I find that the deepest discussions we have about faith in the classroom are always instigated by students, based on the material that we're looking at." Similarly, she also spoke about the importance of the vulnerability that is required for acting, since it "more naturally leads to [faith based] discussions," which can then lead to spiritual maturation. Further, she gave examples of cast members in a production that she directed engaging in discussions about the supernatural with her (as it was related to the production), and about how a study of early theatre history led to discussions with students about "movements that are happening now in terms of social justice [and] in terms of community.... We were able to talk about those in terms of our... responsibility as Christians to the world around us and to our communities." In both cases the conversation developed naturally, and the opportunity was there for her, as the instructor/director, to foster and promote that conversation.

If discussion-oriented instruction was meant to illustrate a flow of verbal traffic between instructor and student, *encouragement* instruction was a one-way street. As the name implies, this type of instruction referred to faculty teaching through the encouragement of a student or group of students. Three of the six faculty made passing references to encouragement as part of their overall pedagogy: F3 stated that she tries to encourage students to realize that they are tougher than they think.

> [Our natural Christian orientation toward belief] should give us an advantage [in storytelling], you know, that Christianity becomes an asset.... We should be courageous. We should be more courageous, not less courageous than our neighbor.... You [the student] know how to believe, don't pretend you don't know how to believe.... And again, I think for the people who aren't Christian, if nothing else I hope it... gives them less sense of a disconnect between faith and theatre.

For her, the ability for the Christian to have a belief in something larger than herself makes her more able to understand the relationship between faith and theatre, and so F3 strives to illuminate that connection to her students. Similarly, if F3 was trying to illuminate the value of faith, F5 understood her role as offering grace and recognition that "some of [the students] are in the midst of that process [of tearing down and rebuilding their faith and] they're not going to have all the answers for themselves." Thus, encouragement for students to continue that rebuilding process was vital for their spiritual health. The same understanding was important for F6 as well, who felt it was important to encourage her students not to hide or abandon their faith when they graduated and entered the professional workforce. She stated, "It is one of the ways we integrate our faith and it is one of the things we teach our kids: when [you] leave here... you don't get to... just be like everybody else in Hollywood.... We are in the public eye, so that's a huge part of integrating your faith is just claiming Christ in situations most people would never do because it's a career killer." Thus her encouragement extended beyond a student's undergraduate career and into their lives after graduation.

The final two types of instruction that were presented in the faculty interviews were organic instruction and structured or formal instruction. Organic instruction includes unforced faith integration that comes about naturally through conversation, shared experiences, or other encounters. It also encompasses an authenticity in its approach to faith integration; it cannot be forced and genuinely expresses the heart of the individuals. Formal instruction is that which is done intentionally on the part of the professor, and usually involves intentional preparation for moments of faith integration that will occur in an upcoming class, production, or meeting. At first it may seem that these two types of instruction are at odds with each other, or that they cannot exist at the same time. In fact, paradoxically, both organic and formal instruction were often mentioned in the same answer by a professor. Though only three of the six professors made references to formal instruction (as compared to five of the six who spoke of organic IFL instruction), all three of them *also* referenced organic instruction as an important part of their IFL teaching. It is also important to note that the other types of instruction already referenced could be done in either an organic or structured fashion (or both). For example, discussion about faith could arise in an organic and natural way during a theatre history class, or a student could discover something new about God or their faith due to a formal, structured approach to acting or script interpretation by a director. Thus, lest a casual reader assume that every professor uses only one method or that each method can only exist if the others are not used, it should be made very clear that these various types of instruction often overlap and are interwoven into the larger fabric of daily pedagogies. In fact, they are rarely so neatly quantified.

Organic instruction was almost always considered to be one, if not *the*, ideal way that faith integration happens in a classroom. F2, F3, F4, F5, and F6 all referenced organic expression of IFL in their answers to the question, "How do you envision the ideal integration of faith and theatre happening in a class?", and F1 hinted at it as well (though not clearly enough for the author to feel comfortable stating it as fact). The general response was that the ideal IFL would "just come up in the class" (F2), that it "has to spring from the moment or it's untenable" (F3), and "in an ideal world it would be more organic, and it would be more instigated by the students" (F4). It wasn't just an ideal for the professors, though, as often it was experienced that way as well. F6 spoke of an experience with a student who was preparing monologues about loss and grief after her own father had passed away, and "taking the organic, authentic moment that's really happening and having the students examine [it to see]... is Christ in that moment?" F2 also spoke of authentic, organic moments, stating, "Mostly it's the subject matter that is the important part because they're paying money for this class, but it's the illumination that comes in [certain] moments [where the ideal faith integration occurs]. It's the flickers of light that weave things together, making connections." And F3 referred to a class where students were writing about their struggles with the Church, and coming to her to hear what she believes on the subject.

Finally, along with organic IFL instruction, three faculty referenced structured or formal instruction. F4 spoke of her faith as "naturally... a part of my daily teaching," but immediately added to that statement by saying she is "required to have a vision based on [faith integration]... and being able to articulate that, I think, is important." This articulation requires a more formal explanation and understanding of the way IFL works, so that she can say why she has done what she did and why she thinks it is effective. F5 spoke of a formal class discussion time when she intentionally created a setting where faith could be discussed, by having students read and discuss playwrights who expressed worldviews contrary to Christianity. And, in the most extensive discussion of formalized instruction, F3 stated that formal instruction was part of the ideal IFL in a production setting because it has to do with the story that she chose and how that story will be told. For her, "there has to be something redemptive and prophetic going on [in the story], even if it's goofy.... [And] it's very important that I'm able to articulate to [the cast] in a formal way, 'This is the story we're telling.'" This formal preparation was important because it then allowed for proper communication between her and the cast, and then between the cast and the audience, to occur. For her, there was an interwoven connection between seeking to change the audience and changing the cast, because if a director cannot tell the cast what their job is ("their job is to serve the audience, their job is to love their audience, not fear them"), then the cast cannot communicate the story and its intention to the audience. Therefore good training, both for herself and for the cast, was essential for faith integration. But at the same time, this formal explanation of the "redemptive and prophetic" elements of the story, and the professional training that comes with it, expressed the organic and integrous nature of the professor who communicated these themes: her organic classroom discussions related to the formal instruction during a production. "You can't teach one thing in a classroom about... 'we don't want to leave people as we found them,' and then, when we're doing the work, suddenly decide that doesn't apply." For her, there had to be internal integrity between instruction and the classroom.

All of these seven modes of instruction (engaged, self-discovery, lecture, discussion, encouragement, organic, and structured or formal) illustrate one of the clusters of meaning related to how faculty perceived faith integration occurring in their department. But instruction was not the only way they understood it. Another way was through *modeling*.

*Modeling*

As with the student and alumni/ae populations, modeling was also mentioned in some form by all of the faculty as a part of the way they perceived and imagined (in the ideal sense) faith integration. However, unlike the students and alumni/ae, faculty generally did not spend very much time talking about modeling. While they seemed to think it had some importance for IFL, it largely had to do with its connection to other clusters of meaning, such as how they taught their students (instruction) or how they viewed themselves (reflexivity).

Four different types of modeling appeared in faculty interviews:

*prayer, organic, interpersonal,* and *study*. All of these are identical, both in substance and in definition, to the categories in the student and alumni/ae data with the same names, but of course here the faculty are talking about themselves, rather than students talking about people in authority.

Only one professor, F1, talked about modeling prayer. As part of the answer to the question, "How do you envision the integration of faith and theatre ideally happening in a class?" this professor gave an example of where she went "shopping with God. [This is] where I have gone out [and] intentionally, prayerfully, asked God before going shopping, laid out what our needs are, and have walked into situations where the perfect thing is there at a ridiculous price and I get it.... I've seen it happen over and over again." This "shopping" was related to theatrical needs, and consequently F1 tells this story to her students when they discuss design, color, or material needs for productions. By presenting such a story, which includes an intentional reference to how to pray, she explains how her faith informs her art. "It's my expression of what I see in how God laid out art and how I follow in that footstep, and I try to be inspired by Him to do my art."

Though more than the single professor who spoke about prayer, only two faculty spoke about modeling an organic approach to IFL, which means that only one-third of the faculty perceived it as meaningful for faith integration, as opposed to two-thirds of the student and alumni/ae participants. These two, F3 and F6, both understood the organic modeling of faith integration as referring to a way of life. For F6, this meant simply doing her job as a teacher, an actor, and a director. It was not something she did at certain times and did not do at other times. As she stated, "Service and who I am are one in the same.... How arrogant of me to decide on focusing on faith now, when He wants me to be doing it all the time." For F3, organic IFL was mentioned slightly differently as it referred to an internal integrity between instruction in the classroom and instruction for the stage. As quoted earlier, she said, "You can't teach one thing in the classroom about... 'we don't want to leave people as we found them,' and then, when we're doing the work [on a production] suddenly decide that doesn't apply." For her, as a model, "faith integration isn't just an afterthought; it's the core of my job." This meant that it should be part of all that she does, from her instruction to her relationships with students and everything in between. Further, she believed this type of organic, integrous modeling was not only important but necessary for faith integration efforts with today's college students.

> This is a generation that can sniff out something disingenuous quicker than any generation ever has. I mean, they see, not a lie but they see a forced moment coming a million miles away. They see an ad, you know what I mean? And they recognize when they're being evangelized, and that that's being kind of like, imposed upon the work.... I have to move in the other direction. There is so much spiritual about what we do, I have to keep myself from talking about it in order to get other stuff taught.

Thus for both F6 and F3 organic modeling had as much to do with their own personal integrity as instructors and as people as it did with the material they taught (perhaps even more so!).

The third type of modeling that was mentioned by faculty was *interpersonal* modeling. As with the students and alumni/ae, this referred to the way faculty understood how they approached their relationships. Three of the six faculty alluded to this type of modeling: F2, F4, and F5. When asked to complete the sentence, "A professor who cares about the spiritual growth of students would never…" F2 added the words, "would never play God with them." By this she meant that she would never "needle" a student about their weaknesses, failures, or personal issues, and that she would not act as if she had all the answers to that student's problems. Rather, she would listen to them, pray with them, and refer them to counseling as appropriate. She felt that by doing this she modeled an interpersonal relationship that was both professional and caring toward the student. F4 said that in order for organic and engaged instruction to occur there must be "safety and openness" in the classroom. This comes about through "the sensitivity of the professor, hopefully, to inclusion of everyone…. I think it's just being sensitive and honoring the students' input into the class and their ideas." This sensitivity and honoring is expressed through simple things, like knowing the students' names, speaking openly and clearly about assignments, and engaging with students respectfully (and getting them to engage with each other in the same way). It also means being "firm about those things that need to be… dealt with, if somebody's being harmful or whatever." When she created a safe environment in the classroom, students could then reasonably expect that they would be safe in approaching her outside of class, and they could take the skills they observed in the classroom and apply them elsewhere as well. Additionally, in a slight departure from the norm, F4 spoke of interpersonal modeling with respect to some of her colleagues. Though she did not call them models, *per se*, she stated that "when people check in, when people pray for you, when people want to know how they could help, rather than just complain, those things are very—I think that reveals the character of your spiritual self." This "character" was modeled through their evident care for her, especially since she and others shared how they were often very busy, which made it "hard to connect" without being intentional about it.

Finally, F5 spoke of interpersonal modeling in two ways. The first had to do with how a faculty member might show care for a student's spiritual growth. In an observation that mirrored many of her colleagues and the author's own experiences, she stated that most students' faith at college goes through a process of deconstruction and reconstruction: they "enter with his or her parent's faith but need to exit with their own." She believed professors should have the grace to recognize that "some of them are in the midst of that process, [and] they're not going to have all the answers for themselves." By doing so, they are modeling a care for the student as a person, not just a receptor for professional knowledge. The second way F5 spoke of interpersonal modeling was through the intentional way she tried to live and tried to teach her students to live.

> People are drawn to people who are of faith…. I think Madeline L'Engle says we draw to Christ by showing them a light so warm and bright that they want to know its source…. One way that Christ followers… can identify themselves and set themselves apart is by what they say. Can you

not engage in gossip with everybody else? Can you be edifying, not destructive, with your words? Can you not use foul language, unless something really, really goes wrong?... One of my favorite authors used to talk about going on airplanes and trying to decide, "How soon do I tell people I'm a Christian?" And his decision is, "Let me wait, and then they can decide if they like me first before I bring that up."

Thus this second reference to interpersonal modeling was largely about personal behavior as a means of expressing personal belief, in the hope that it might lead to conversations about faith. Clearly this type of modeling is closely connected to organic modeling as well.

The final type of modeling that the faculty made reference to was the modeling of *study,* specifically how the professors demonstrated the importance of study for both professional and spiritual maturation. Three of the six faculty mentioned this type of modeling. F2 presented it as largely an exercise in preparation. For her, modeling existed in how she came prepared to work with students. This might have been through "sourcing a quote from Kierkegaard" to illustrate what is done with actors, or it may have been by modeling professionalism and knowledge about the subject matter surrounding her job on a production. F3 understood the modeling of study as it related to her interpretation and direction of a production:

> Directing [a particular show] was a way of being able to articulate [and]... understand the prophetic value of theatre, as [theologian Walter] Brueggemann would use that term.... You are speaking truth to power. I mean, if the prophetic function is to speak truth to power and to do it in the cause of the oppressed.... And you know, I looked at my students and I saw they were helpless and harassed like sheep without a shepherd... in the culture that was surrounding them.... I remember the three students who played the leading player, and I remember them breaking down on several occasions because [of] the lines [that] were coming out of their mouth, they understood it had been directed at them, culturally for years and years and years, and for a while they couldn't get through the lines.

F3's directorial choices, which included highlighting the "prophetic" voice of the production in a way that allowed it to speak a counter-narrative to the culture in which her student actors found themselves, allowed the students to discover a perspective that illuminated the lies of the world and brought them to tears because of the spiritual, emotional, and even physical freedom that it delivered. This could only have happened because she knew the play, knew the message that she wanted to convey, and had communicated that knowledge to the cast and crew.

Finally, F1 understood the modeling of study as occurring through how she turned to God for creativity and inspiration. Being "connected" to God gave her access to a larger creativity and another perspective to "collaborate" with on theatrical projects. She sought to share this collaborative approach with students as they studied various techniques, and she would tell stories about times when she felt God give her divine inspiration for production designs. One such example was a production of *Waiting for Godot* at another university, an existential piece with a theme that some have interpreted to be "God's not coming.... God's not really there, really, is kind of the message of the piece." Through prayerful "collaboration" F1 had the idea to have a large, Godlike hand holding the stage on which the actors of the show would perform, thus changing the message of the show: now instead of "God's not coming" the theme shifted to humanity's willful ignorance of God's presence and provision. Another example was when she saw Arthur Miller's original notes written into the margins of *The Crucible*, a play about the Salem witch trials that many have taken to be a social commentary about McCarthy-ism. Though this interpretation may be partially correct, these original notes referred to spiritual warfare. Consequently, in her production (also at another university) she chose to "put some demons on stage and they were talking into ears of people during the trial… to show the unseen… spiritual realm." These examples were presented both to the author and to F1's students as illustrations of modeling study in a manner that seeks to integrate faith with theatrical design and direction.

These four types of modeling (prayer, organic, interpersonal and study) encompass how the faculty at this university's theatre department perceived or imagined faith integration happening within this cluster of meaning. As stated earlier, however, it is important to note that the references to modeling by the faculty were far fewer than they were in the student and alumni/ae interviews. This will be addressed in the next chapter, where the results of all the data are discussed in greater detail. In the interim, however, we must move on to the next cluster of meaning put forth by the faculty, *identity*.

*Identity*

Identity was a category unique to the faculty participants. As the name suggests, it largely deals with how faculty understand their own character. This understanding appeared in two different ways throughout the interviews: their identity in relation to others, and their own self-awareness irrespective of others. These two facets of self-perception affected how the faculty experienced faith integration in their own lives.

F2 was one of only two faculty participants who spoke of her faith deepening because of a personal connectivity with others. When asked how she has changed during her time as a professor at the university, she stated that she believed her faith had grown stronger and deeper because she was allowed to work in an area that she was passionate about and that allowed her to integrate her own faith into the classroom. "[H]ere, to be with people where they *get it* and both [faith and art] can work together, has helped my faith grow" (emphasis original). Part of "getting it" was illustrated by her relationship with one of the other professors who "talked about [faith] a lot" with her. These two professors share "on a heart to heart level" and have a shared "understanding" of each other as equals, both professionally and spiritually. In the same way, F3 also shared about a relationship she had with a faculty member that allowed for discussion of faith. Thus the environment in which F2 and F3 found themselves allowed them to develop in their own spiritual growth.

The other type of identity that came up during the interviews was self-awareness or self-identity. Five of the six faculty made some reference to this during our time together, and it was understood by each of them to be an important part of how they perceived faith integration within their own lives.

All five professors found their identity in their standing as Christ followers. F1 believed that her faith was "central to everything we do" and affected her "approach [to] storytelling" and her worldview. Consequently, she sought to model her work after how God worked in Scripture, and to use the gifts that she felt had been given to her by God. She stated, "I am a child of God as [much as] somebody who's a big fancy theologian, and God made me as a designer." Further, "I think if we get back to that idea that we're Christians called with whatever gifts we're given, whether you're a lawyer or an accountant or, you know, a businessman or whatever you are, if you are following God in that pursuit, that's where you need to be." So for F1 there was an understanding that God determines people to be certain types of workers or have certain orientations (such as artistic bents), and that this is so God can use the skill sets in these people for whatever purposes God deems appropriate. Similarly, F3 understood her standing as a Christian to affect her own worldview as well, which included how she treats people, her view of self as a sinner, and the knowledge that she is an eternal being. This worldview then affected how she taught her subject and lived out her calling as an artist. As she stated, "Faith integration isn't just an afterthought, it's the core of my job. But… faith integration integrates a number of things," and it manifests in multiple ways, including how she sought out "prophetic" pieces to direct, how she interacted with and treated students and colleagues, and how she sought to live an integrated life that embodied the principles and messages she taught in the classroom. F6 sought to not separate "who we are from when we're at work," and she understood "being an actor and being a Christian" as both compatible and holistically integrated because her faith was a way of living. F5 also found that her identity as a Christian informs what she does. "As a person of faith I believe that it should somehow inform the art that I create in some shape, form or fashion." But she was quick to point out that she viewed herself as an artist who happens to be Christian, not as a Christian artist; her artistic talents are not (foremost) a means of sharing her faith, but rather her faith informed her overall approach to doing the artistic work that she was gifted in. And, like her colleagues, F4 said that having a "Christ-like" integrity was very important to her understanding of self and how effective she thought her efforts were at faith integration. Interestingly though, in addition to this she found that her role as a professor played a part in her own growth, very similar to what F2 mentioned above. She stated that students "force me to think about [faith's relation to art] every day in the questions they ask," and when she directs a show it forces her to think about faith's relation to the piece in order to be able to talk to students and audience members about it during rehearsals and talkbacks. So for her, being at a Christian university has "fundamentally helped me grow into an understanding of what I do and why I do it." F5 also stated a similar awareness of growth because of her teaching. "Because you're going through this process [of examining faith in relation to your craft] continually with your students, I'm a lot more settled than I was… years ago when I started teaching."

*Mentoring*

The fourth cluster of meaning that the faculty identified as being important for faith integration was *mentoring*. This category largely followed the same lines as was discussed in the student and alumni/ae populations: both intentional mentoring and *in situ* mentoring were understood to be significant, though many times the line was blurry between the two categories. Further, only two of the six felt it was important enough for them to engage in formal, stated mentoring relationships with students (though mentoring in the generic, *in situ* sense was brought up by four of the six faculty).

F4 and F1 spoke most forthrightly about mentoring, particularly as it related to being intentional in their mentoring relationships with students. For both of them, this correlated to their care for students' overall well-being and spiritual growth. F4 had intentionally mentored some students and still met with those who had graduated. F1 had done the same. "I consider myself to be tied together [with students] as a mentor for their life," she said, adding,

> During productions I spend more time with my students than I do with my family. And they become my family. I mean, I adopt—no joke, we've had so many kids that have gone through our programs at the different schools I've been at that I consider to be my adopted, you know, sons and daughters. We did a cross-country trip this summer, and it was a vacation, but we made part of our vacation, three days of our vacation, to attend a wedding of a former student. And to see some other former students that attended the wedding as well. We stayed a couple nights, independent of this, with some other former students that are older and married and have kids now and stuff. We dropped in, they had us stay in the guest room and we'd hang out with them. It's not just, you know, here's your four years and we hand you a certificate, or diploma, go away. I consider myself to be tied together as a mentor for their life. I mean, obviously I'm not going to see them as much as I do when they're here, but I want to know what's going on with them, I want to know how they're doing five or ten years down the road. And I think that's what's unique about being at a Christian university, I think there's a different level of depth to that.

This type of "adoption" by F1 may continue well beyond students' college years, but they begin while working together at the university. F6 spoke of a student whose father had recently passed away, and how, through working with the professor on monologues about abandonment and death, she was better able to deal with the loss and see how God took something bad and brought some good out of it. F4 referred to a student with whom she had several discussions about a role the student was playing. The actor "has to curse God [and] there were a lot of opportunities for us to talk about the implications of that for the actor, and what the audience needed to get, separation of actor from character, [etc.]." She also spoke about other *in situ* opportunities she had where students asked about character motivations or actions. In such instances, "that's a question about themselves, not about that character," and it provided an opportunity "to engage the student on a deeper level." Those types of situations provided space to discuss spiritual matters, but also required a lot of discernment on her part. "Are they just tired because they're in a production? Is this an opportunity for me…?" But, she said, most importantly, "I have to say the Holy Spirit is present in many of those situations. Theatre is all about listening for the subtext."

F2 referred to several experiences with students who came to her in order to improve their professional skills, but who ended up needing or desiring *in situ* mentoring in the process. "The problem with the subject matter is whenever you're working on something, stuff comes out. So I'm really quick to tell everyone I'm not a psychologist or a counselor, not trained. I don't want to mess with that, so when issues come up I more just pray with someone and then say, 'Would you like to go to the Counseling Center?' That sounds like a joke, it's not actually. I *would* like to pass them on to people who are trained for that kind of thing." But, she adds, "I *do* pray with students in those settings. A lot." Finally, F6 told the author that her office seemed to be the place where students who questioned their faith or felt like outsiders came for guidance. In her understanding, her job made her like a therapist, because students were naturally comfortable coming to her since she worked so closely with them on difficult internal emotions and issues related to the craft of acting. This even applied to non-theatre majors as well.

Obviously mentoring was perceived to be an important part of how some faculty understood faith integration within their department. But if their instruction, their personal sense of self-identity, their modeling, and their mentoring were the external, visible parts of faith integration, then the final two clusters of meaning demonstrated that these activities could not stand on their own.

*Preparation*

The fifth cluster of meaning that arose from the faculty conversations was *preparation*. This refers to the things that faculty did outside of the purview of the students that they deemed important for the success of their faith integration efforts. These things were always understood to be related to their profession (both as professors and as working professionals) and also related to spiritual preparation for their work as faith-based educators.

Within the preparation cluster three different types of preparation were identified. However, two of the three types were only clearly evident in the interview from *one* faculty member, F1: *prayer* and *accountability*. Thus, though they are important and worth mentioning here, and though it is likely that many (if not all) of the other professors engaged in these preparatory techniques, it must be noted that the data does not support these as having a perceived significant influence across the board.

For F1, prayer was understood to be an essential part of the personal preparation process for faith integration. For her, being "open to hearing God's voice" was vital for her own creative processes, as it allowed her to tap into a creativity that was larger than her own. "[I]f I'm not connected to God directly through the process, I'm going with whatever limited things I have in my box at the moment," which limits the effectiveness of her work. "Faith is connected to everything I do.... If my relationship with God is in order, it is automatically going to flow into my profession." Further, prayer from others was a sign of care and valuing of her own contributions to the faculty effort, and she appreciated being at a university where they prayed for each other.

On a related note, F1 also spoke about accountability as important for her own personal preparation. She related that the university has "a very intentional system in place to keep you focused on what you're doing" with respect to IFL, and for her this was "refreshing." Additionally, the faculty within the department, and within the university as a whole, modeled a faith that is "sincerely seeking the Lord.... [I]t's not the administration doing this, it's more of the community looking at one another and encouraging one another." This encouragement, along with the "intentional system," were understood to be a great source of spiritual accountability for F1, which fostered a continuing desire to integrate her faith into everything that she did.

The third type of preparation, which was shared among five of the six faculty, was study. Just as faculty modeling of good study habits and applications was perceived as a way for students to develop their own abilities, so too was being properly prepared for faith integration moments through the practice of study deemed important. This was expressed during the interviews in various ways. For F1 this meant that she felt the need to give an accurate representation of Scripture. "I think in order to be a good Christian professor you need to understand the Word of God.... There can be some room and leeway for disagreement or differences of opinion on noncritical issues... but on the key, core tenets of Christianity I have to be very clear about that because I think I'm responsible to God for that, to communicate that clearly." Therefore, in order to do this she must continue to study Scripture and determine its application to her work. For F2, preparation was essential for her to do her best work. This meant studying the play, studying the characters, and understanding the probable needs of the actors who would be playing those roles. For her, faith was part of who she was and her approach to the job, not an external event or thing. As she put it, "The only way I can talk about integrating my faith in a production level, to me, is in the preparation. In the thinking through things before.... It's who you're bringing to it. It's in the preparation."

F3 spoke extensively about study as a form of preparation for faith integration. In her case it largely had to do with the shows she chose to direct and the way the stories would be told. But it also manifested in how she then interpreted and saw shows and characters, such as viewing Don Quixote as a "Christ-figure," or Charles Dickens's *Christmas Carol* as a "cautionary play." She naturally began seeing these things because her faith perspective naturally trained her to think this way. Like F1, F4 also saw her own study as important for her efforts at faith integration, and this study included both Bible study and "the ability to understand the literature in [the] field" that related to faith integration. Sometimes this literary examination was necessitated by the university, and other times it was brought on by student questions or the desire to prepare for audience questions after a performance. In either case, however, she expressed that "those things that make you articulate what you believe are really, really important, and not many places do that like university does." Finally, F5 understood study preparation as necessary for her own ability to converse with students on topics related to faith, as well as being vital for the creation of courses that had strong faith integration components. She gave the example of a proposed interdisciplinary "faith-and-film type course, not unlike what Rob Johnston has done at Fuller [Theological Seminary] with Reel Spirituality, looking at films from a Biblical worldview." Though it found expression in different ways, all five of these faculty highlighted the importance of study in their preparation to address matters of faith integration, even if their efforts were never immediately known by the students.

*Motivation*

Just as faculty preparation was not always seen by students, so too the factors that motivated faculty to teach in a manner that promoted faith integration were not always seen. All six of the faculty expressed multiple factors that motivated them in their efforts to integrate faith into their chosen subjects. The motivations that appeared in the interviews were *evangelism, faith preparation, connectivity with others, professional training,* and *purpose.*

Four of the six faculty spoke about what this author terms evangelism as a motivating factor in their efforts to integrate faith and learning. This term has a loaded history within theological studies, but for our purposes it refers to the idea of theatre as *ministry*, a way to share elements of one's Christian faith with others through the act of storytelling and/or through working together on a shared project with a shared goal. These "others" may be audience members, members of the cast or crew, or those who have some interaction with the faculty in a more peripheral way (e.g., outside renters, builders, or designers). F1 summed it up this way: "[O]ne of the things that is so important about faith integration is... I think that we get into this idea, like the Church, where only the clergy are allowed to minster, and that's not the way it's supposed to be.... [T]he clergy are supposed to equip the believers, and the Church is supposed to go out then and they're supposed to be the ministers wherever they are." Theatre practitioners are supposed to be ministers in their field, a field that is "not an easy place to be" as a Christian. "I think if we get back to that idea that we're Christians called with whatever gifts we're given... if you are following God in that pursuit, and letting God inspire you in that pursuit, and sharing your faith as you go through that pursuit, that's where you need to be." Thus F1 was motivated by her efforts to share her faith with others, a motivation that existed both at the university and before it, when, because of her unique talents, she was able to share her faith with colleagues while designing and creating monster makeup. Her hope now as a professor is that her students might go out, work in the industry, illuminate the messages within art to others, and teach others how to analyze art in a missional way where they can share their faith as well.

In the same vein, F3 also was motivated by an evangelistic predisposition. For her, all the productions she sought to work on were meant to be "redemptive and prophetic." This was important because she understood the power and the privilege of being a storyteller. As she put it, the ideology of the storyteller "is embedded in our stories, and… audiences are most open to having their minds changed when they're being entertained because they're not defending themselves." Thus the stories that she and her students told required an intentional focus and purpose, which was to point their audiences (and selves) back to Christ and Christ's work in the world.

> The main thing is Christ. And everything else comes after. The main thing is Gospel. It's just so easy for the gospel to get lost in… a society which, I believe, is both moralizing and immoral…. If I care about a student's spiritual development it's really important for me to let them know, "It isn't about you, Christ does all the heavy lifting. You're along for the ride." And that goes for unbelievers as well, who are like, "I don't know why but I just can't believe it." I'm like, "Faith comes from God, stick around. That's His job too."

Thus the telling of "redemptive and prophetic" stories was an important way to highlight the ills of society and present a faithful alternative that places the weight of the work on God's doing.

F5 hinted at an evangelistic motivation in her interview as well. As stated in the section on interpersonal modeling, F5 spoke of the author Madeline L'Engle, who said, "we draw people to Christ by showing them a light so warm and bright that they want to know its source" (as quoted by F5). This quote motivated her to live a life that exemplified her Christian faith, and it also motivated her to encourage her students to do likewise, especially in their work. In her interview she spoke of two different ways to tell a story, "the Aristotelian model and the Platonic model." The Platonic model is prescriptive: "This is how you should live your life," and according to F5 it usually does not make for good art or storytelling. The Aristotelian model is descriptive: "This is what happens when you don't do the right thing," and it's from this model that we get Shakespeare, the tragic flaw in storytelling, and morality plays "where somebody is allowed to make a mistake and we get to see the ramifications of it." She gave *Breaking Bad* as a contemporary television example of this model. "People need to see an example, positive or negative, but they need to see it played out." While she admits it can backfire as a method of storytelling, such as when people don't learn from the mistake or when they exalt the sin/wrong, for her, great storytelling is when "somebody wants something badly and something else is preventing him from getting it," and the Aristotelian model allows for this type of story more easily. She presented this in order to illustrate how storytelling, and knowing the proper and most effective ways to tell stories in contemporary culture, can be a way to communicate the truthfulness of the gospel (and its subsequent morality) to the world in ways that nonbelievers are willing to listen to. Thus, though it was not explicitly stated in her interview, this author believes that a heart for ministry served as partial motivation for the work of this particular professor.

This same heart was also present in F6, who said that theatre "is a place where God lives. It is a place where He's doing His work." Consequently, good storytelling is a way of impacting the world for God by creating a vehicle for the story that God wants to tell and then letting God do the rest. "I think that to tell His story, tell His truths, will make an impact in the world greatly.... Christians just have to quit making mediocre films and [telling] mediocre stories. And they have to start making stories that the story itself is great.... [W]e're not on a missionary message, but... all truth is God's truth, [and that is] being revealed. And God will do the rest for you." The phrase "missionary message" referred to an earlier comment in the interview about how God uses more than just "Billy Graham" to impact the world, and though it seems to contradict her point, the overall answers to the questions posed to her indicated that she felt her work as a theatre professor was a way for her to teach Christian students how to tell stories well in order that they might be "a walking testimony" to how God has worked (and is working) in the world. Indeed, she even obliquely referred to her task as "mission work" when she spoke about the challenges of faith integration for actors, since they usually don't write the scripts that they perform.

> We [as actors] are breathing life into them. We are not writing an article or a book. As our integration of faith we are taking in an existing story with a collaborative amount of people, not a solo journey, working together as a unit to tell a human story for Christ. It's a totally different animal than a lot of different mission work; it's not as "on the nose."

Thus, even though F6 did not see theatre work (and acting in particular) as being "on the nose" missional or evangelistic, it was still a "different" kind of mission, one that sought to illuminate God and God's work in the world through the authentic telling of the story.

Very closely related to evangelism was the motivation of *faith preparation*. If the end goal was that students would one day go out into the entertainment industry and share their faith with others (either through stories or through more direct conversations), the more immediate goal of the faculty was to ensure that students' faith was an integral part of their collegiate theatre experiences while with them at university. This was so important that it was mentioned in some fashion by all six faculty participants.

Because F1 understood faith as something that gives "us the meaning for life," helping students understand their faith in relation to their art helped to provide that overall sense of meaning in both her life and theirs. "[M]y desire to teach at a Christian university [relates to] the fact that I am open to share my faith... and hopefully help in nurturing upcoming designers and actors and people that are going to be working in that field." This nurturing existed in many forms, such as instruction, mentoring, and modeling faith, and always had a two-pronged focus.

> I'm teaching them how to be professionals in their field, but I'm also preparing them for some of the challenges, and in many ways it is kind of like a missions field... where we can approach people, we speak their language. The specific language of theatre, we understand all that.... And

so talking to them about it, "Okay, if you're working in film, they don't recognize weekends as anything, so you're not going to be able to go to Church every Sunday, you realize that. If you aren't, [then] how are you going to be spiritually fed?"... "If you're in a place where, you know, 98 percent of the people, 99 percent of the people are not Christians, it's real easy to get drawn into all their stuff. Are you going to have people that are behind you praying? Behind the scenes, that are supporting you?"... That kind of stuff is really important to share with students.

Thus faith preparation in this instance had both professional and spiritual elements which were seen to complement each other.

F2 thought that the "openness to wonder" and searching that the acting experience awakens in students was one of the reasons why faith integration was beneficial, but IFL also "gives some understanding and some scope to the real human depravity." It therefore can be a tool to prevent people from "soaring like a God" and becoming too egocentric, thus shaping them into a more humble actor whose humility can serve as a beacon of the Christian faith in a profession full of self-important people. Similarly, since F3 also understood theatre as having the capacity to "affect what people believe," she understood her job as not only teaching about and directing shows that have "redemptive and prophetic" messages but also instructing and providing opportunities for students to look for these things themselves in order that they might maintain that ability once they begin working professionally. This, then, provided a means for showing students that their faith, and the perspective it brings, is an asset for theatre work that those without faith do not have. As she put it, Christians "are people of story. We should be better at this than anyone because we are believers, we're trained to keep believing. And so, it comes up a lot for me, how naturally this should give us an advantage, you know, that Christianity becomes an asset. And of you don't take advantage of your assets, all you're left with are the liabilities." This asset can then lead to a "courage" that stands apart from the self-consciousness of most actors and provides a motivation to continue being a confident Christian in a difficult profession.

If F2 understood faith as a way to remain humble, and F3 saw it as means to impart courage in her students, F4, F5, and F6 were simply motivated to allow students to continue in their respective faith journeys. F4 said, "I think we always need to be sensitive that everyone's on their faith journey, and not everybody aligns with the same way of framing Christian ideas.... We are a Christian institution, we all hold to the mission, and the students, they're aware, but within that I think we can be a little sensitive to maybe finding different ways of approaching faith integration." One should not take this as "live and let live" however, for even though sensitivity was important, more than anything else she wanted "our students to graduate and impact the world for Christ." Thus she spoke extensively about mentoring, modeling, and different types of instruction that sought to prepare students to think critically about their faith and its relation to their faith. For her, faith preparation was still a very important part of her profession, it just occurred in more personal and informal ways. F5 was much the same, stating that professors needed to have grace with their students to recognize that "some of them are in the midst of [a deconstruction and reconstruction] process [in their faith], and they're not going to have all the answers for themselves." Consequently, faith preparation largely occurred in how she modeled and included her own faith in her classroom instruction. And for F6, faith preparation meant creating a safe place for students to question their beliefs or work through life issues. "If we don't leave the door open for them to question the validity of God and whether or not this is real, and whether or not they're allowed to question Him, then we shut the door to them having an authentic relationship with Him." This open-door approach meant that F6 served, in some fashion, like a de facto therapist, letting students talk through issues, pray about/for them, and vent their concerns in a way that both affirmed their experiences and the fact that God was still in control. "That's the time I start saying, 'It's okay. It's okay for you to question…. He's got you. He's there whether you know it or not. He's still around.'… It's okay just to let them know that God—'it's alright and just hang with it and you'll work it out. And I'm not judging you and I'm sorry you feel that people are [judging you] and God loves you and so do I.'" The purpose of this type of openness and responsiveness was that F6 believed it would allow students to be used by God to tell the stories that God wanted to be told, and it would one day allow them to tell others their story, their "testimony," in a way that was truthful.

As it was important for the faculty to see their students grow in their relationship with God, a few were motivated to pursue faith integration in order that their own faith and *connectivity with God* might continue to grow as well. F1 spoke of God as her source of creativity and inspiration, and how being "connected" to God gave her access to a larger creativity and another perspective to "collaborate" with. "Faith is connected to everything I do…. If my relationship with God is in order, it's automatically going to flow into my profession." F6 also spoke of faith integration as important for her faith, largely because, for her, "being an actor and being a Christian" were the same thing. Thus, in her understanding, her faith naturally came through her professional and instructional work, and, conversely, through the theatrical process she learned more about God. As she put it, "Anything that is… driven in truth and… compelled [by] honesty, Christ is in." Further, "I think most theatre artists that are Christians see [the theatre] as a place for God's work to happen whether or not we're doing Christian plays." Thus theatre could be a place for God to work and reveal truth, where God could find her instead of the other way around.

Just as some faculty saw faith integration as a way to grow in relation to God, others saw it as a means to grow more *connected with others*. Faculty were motivated to pursue IFL because it drew them closer to each other, closer to the students, and closer to the larger community. F3 spoke of a close relationship she had with a fellow faculty member, with whom faith discussions happened often. F4 also sought to engage with her fellow faculty about faith ("I am constantly trying to find ways to foster that kind of connection—I think it is essential."), but she also understood her work as a translator of sorts, someone who could "contextualize" plays for the students, the university, and the surrounding community in order that they might engage more fully in the IFL happening within productions. F5 shared about a production that she directed that helped her, as well as many of the cast, to better relate to friends and family who had gone through difficult divorces. And F6 saw herself and her fellow faculty as having the "same mission," which included an "element of service" to the students, service that allowed for deeper relationships than could be had at a secular institution. She also wanted to see a class added to the program that dealt with ministry and had a purpose more aligned with "building community and less about everybody sitting down and being entertained."

If overt spiritual care was evident in the motivation of the faculty, both for themselves and for the students in particular, nearly all the faculty were equally motivated by the desire to provide *professional training* to their students, as well. Interestingly, though perhaps not surprisingly, the entire faculty understood this professional preparation as being intimately connected with students' spiritual preparation, and the two were nearly always mentioned together in some fashion. F1 said that faith "centers" the decision-making process for an artist, and the decisions which were presented as examples all related to professional, theatrical endeavors. She also saw her job as *both* teaching students to be professional and competent in their work, *and* preparing them for the challenge of being Christian in a largely secular environment. Similarly, F2 stated that her job was to help students achieve professional growth, but this was done by having a trust-based relationship with the students that allowed for organic faith integration to occur. Both F3 and F5 were motivated to train professionals who were excellent storytellers so that they could go out and "change" (F3) the minds of audiences about Christian faith and God, and provide "examples" (F5) of right or wrong ways to live. In fact, F5 said that "as a director that can be your proudest moment, when you can accurately capture… what the playwright intended" and show the truthfulness of humanity in ways that prompt conversations of faith. Further, F5 believed that the professional training of artists was vital because the "intellectual property economy is 90 percent larger than the US manufacturing economy" and is currently the largest export of the United States, and thus training students who can contribute to that "intellectual property" is important for their own futures. But she quickly returned to the sentiment that "our job as educators is to help students discern their vocational calling" and that the calling may not have much bearing on their jobs, or not in the way a student initially thinks. She gave the example of some alumni/ae who were using their experience to train

> people in recovery from substance abuse, homelessness, and mental illness to make films and [put] them to work on commercial projects…. So the skills we teach them… can be used directing for the Kingdom or in the mission field that is Hollywood, influencing people for the Kingdom. But God will make their path known to them as they go on through, but we can't stop them.

Finally, F6 said that it was important that shows be chosen that would train students to go out into the profession and "make an impact for Christ," which included shows that "deal with real issues that are contemporary and [that]… still reveal the truth for God, and show the reflections of humanity truthfully, and do not celebrate poor choices but reveal poor choices for humanity [in order] to influence an audience not to make them, and celebrate redemptive moments in the stories."

This type of training, and the inclusion of material that is not overtly Christian or faith-based, could allow students to compete at the highest levels because that material might meet an educational need. But even still, she added that the cast's "job is to find that humanity of that character and to use themselves as an instrument for God to tell that story so it's His call whether or not He's making an impact." Thus, even in productions that seem to have no faith component, the faculty felt that they were training professionals who could find God in anything (or create space for God to work in anything).

The last motivational factor, and perhaps the culmination of what has come before, is *purpose*. Faith integration gave purpose to what the faculty were doing. All of the other motivations sum up their stated purpose: to prepare students to pursue good art from a Christian perspective in order to change the landscape of the profession in a positive way, a way where Christians create the best art precisely because of their faith. This purpose (to prepare) encompasses their desires to prepare students spiritually and professionally, to send them out as "ministers" of the gospel into the industry, and to connect with God and others. Though this purpose manifested in different ways it undergirded all that was done by the faculty: "reflect[ing] humanity truthfully" (F6); teaching students that their faith "should somehow inform the art" (F5); having students "impact the world for Christ" because of the collaborative and rigorous nature of the department (F4); teaching students to be "better... people of story... than anyone because we're believers" and this is their asset (F3); and "combin[ing] your faith and your profession" (F1) all gave a sense of purpose and direction to how the faculty approached their respective theatrical crafts. As F1 put it, "If we're not going to have aspects about how to combine your faith and your profession, how to live that out, why are we here as a Christian university? That's what is unique about us."

## Negative IFL

As was presented in chapter three, the last section of data that is important to mention here is not so much a cluster of meaning as it is a cluster of significance. Two of the questions posed to participants asked what a professor who integrates faith and learning (or who cares for a student's spiritual growth) would *not* do. The purpose of these questions was to determine what the various participants perceived of as having a negative effect on a student's spiritual growth or understanding of their faith. These responses largely followed in line with what was expounded upon in other answers (or they serve to provide the negative expression of those answers). Sometimes faculty spoke of negative influences within other answers as well. The actual breakdown of responses is as follows:

F1: "Somebody who is... practicing good faith integration would never give an inaccurate representation of Scripture." Further, this professor would never "lead them astray from God's truth in the Bible," which requires a genuine relationship with students in order to provide accountability and a caring space for growth to occur.

F2: A professor who cares about the integration of faith and learning would never "just do Bible studies in class for five minutes." Faith integration must be more organic and more interwoven into the fabric of the course itself, and rubrics that try to evaluate faith integration efforts do not allow for this type of integration. Further, a professor who cares about his or her students would never "play God with them" and act as if they have all the answers to a student's questions, but would rather ensure they were sent to qualified, appropriate care.

F3: A professor who cares about the integration of faith and learning "would never have to force that" because it is inherently part of who they are. Some efforts can be too formal or evidence-based, which shows a misunderstanding of faith integration in the arts and can lead to an atmosphere of fear, which inhibits a desired, organic kind of integration. For F3, a professor's faith should naturally come through their instruction. Also, a professor who cares about the spiritual growth of their students "would never take their eyes off the main thing. The main thing is Christ. And everything else comes after." By having this focus, care for students and a desire for IFL will organically take place.

F4: A professor who cares about the integration of faith and learning would never "dismiss a student because they don't align with that faith.... [W]e always need to be sensitive that everyone's on their own journey, and not everybody aligns with the same way of framing Christian ideas." But importantly, caring about a student's spiritual growth means never missing "an opportunity to discuss it," and being willing "to engage the students on a deeper level." With this type of discussion-based, organic faith integration, specific faith integration assignments were felt to be a negative influence (she had students who called it the "Jesus assignment" because, "they know it's put on.").

F5: A professor who cares about the integration of faith and learning would never "disparage a student's beliefs or hold him or her as a subject of ridicule." For F5 this also applies to their abilities as a theatre practitioner, not just their faith. Further, just as a professor should not mock a student's faith, they also should never "do anything to stifle that growth," which requires acknowledging that they do not have all the answers to life's questions.

F6: A professor who cares about the integration of faith and learning "would never determine what is faith-based and what is not. Because they understand that in the arts... everything... belongs to God if it's based in truth." Consequently, since a professor would never make such a determination they also would never "allow [or] make an environment where [students are] not allowed to question or even challenge their faith.... If we don't leave the door open for them to question the validity of God and whether or not this is real and whether or not they're allowed to question Him, then we shut the door to them having an authentic relationship with Him." Like the other professors, F6 valued an organic, relational approach to faith integration, which meant that she felt structured faith integration assignments were unhelpful and that the students themselves should be the rule by which faculty are assessed.

It should also be noted that four of the six faculty members mentioned *busyness*, which included their workload, as a negative influence on their ability to integrate faith into their instruction. This is not surprising, given that all of them spoke effulgently about the value of relational, organic faith integration within their department, and busyness would naturally prevent such relationships from forming at the level required for meaningful conversations and interactions.

So what do all of these responses mean, exactly? What can be drawn from them? Or to return again to the phenomenological nature of our study, what is the "essence" of how both groups, the students and alumni/ae and the faculty, perceived and imagined faith integration? Let us now turn our attention to these very questions.

# Interpretation of Findings

In the previous two chapters data were presented that had been collected from the interviews with students, alumni/ae, and faculty at the university chosen for this study. This data sought to capture the responses given to questions related to perceptions and envisioned ideals of the integration of faith and learning (IFL) within the university's theatre department. When the data were coded and analyzed, various categories and groupings began to emerge. Initially placed into "in vivo" groups (groups that are named using the actual language of the participants),[1] these categories eventually evolved into what was covered in chapters three and four: for the students and alumni/ ae, *mentoring, modeling, preparation, motivation* and *connectivity*; and for the faculty, *instruction, modeling, identity, motivation*, and *mentoring*. These categories have been richly expounded upon already, so there is no need to rehash them in detail here.

But now we must return to the original questions asked in this study: how do students and faculty imagine IFL ideally happening, and how do they perceive it actually happening now? Properly divided up, there are four distinct questions to answer: (1) How do students imagine the ideal integration of faith and learning happening in their program? (2) How do faculty imagine the ideal integration of faith and learning happening in their department? (3) How do students perceive effective IFL in their program? (4) How do faculty perceive their IFL efforts? Further, these two groups, students and faculty, should then be compared in order to see if student imaginings of IFL have points of similarity or discord with faculty imaginings. This chapter will attempt to answer these questions and make the comparison between the two major groups. And, because this is a phenomenological study, it will also craft statements that describe the *essence* of student and faculty ideals and perceptions. The best way to do this, now that the data have been examined on a micro scale, is to step back and discover the larger picture. For example, how do the various clusters of meaning compare to each other? Or, how do the student and alumni/ae data compare with the faculty data?

The next several pages will be laid out in the following way: first will be a summary of how students imagined the *ideal* integration of faith and learning happening in the program.[2] Then will follow a summary of how faculty imagined IFL ideally happening in their department. After the two summaries, points of convergence and commonality between the two groups will be explored. This exploration will culminate in textual and structural descriptions that describe *what*

---

[1] Creswell, *Research Design*, 192.

[2] From this point forward, in order to allow for a more streamlined process both current students and alumni/ae of the department will be lumped together and referred to as "students." Where necessary and appropriate, differences between current students and alumni/ae will be highlighted, but their general experiences were similar enough to allow these groups to merge for our purposes.

was imagined and *how* it was imagined. From this will come an *essence* statement that seeks to illustrate and "[typify] the experiences of all the participants in the study."[3] Once this has been accomplished, this same sequence of events will repeat and focus on the *perceptions* of IFL. The chapter will then conclude with some thoughts.

## Student IFL Ideals

As part of the interview process, students were asked four questions that sought to illuminate their understanding of how faith integration should ideally happen in the learning experience:

(1) *If you were a professor, how would you integrate faith and theatre in a class?*

(2) *If you were a professor, how would you integrate faith and theatre in a production that you were in charge of?*

(3) *Please finish this sentence: A professor who integrates faith and learning would never...?*

(4) *Please finish this sentence: A professor who cares about my/a student's spiritual growth would never...?*

These questions were developed in part to better engage the two distinct learning environments where students and faculty regularly interact within the department (the classroom and the stage), but also to maintain some continuity with the Sherr, Huff, and Curran study from 2007,[4] which first prompted the idea for this study. The answers to these questions are below.

Among the student populations that were interviewed, four different clusters of meaning were identified as being part of the ideal way that faith integration would exist in a classroom setting, and within those four clusters of meaning there were a total of eleven categories:

| | |
|---|---|
| **Mentoring:**<br>- In Situ<br><br>**Modeling:**<br>- Decision Making<br>- Interpersonal<br>- Valuing<br>- Organic/Integrous IFL<br>- Prayer (Practices)<br>- Study (Practices) | **Preparation:**<br>- Prayer<br>- Study<br><br>**Motivation:**<br>- Purpose<br>- Service |

Similarly, within the production settings students identified five clusters of meaning with eleven categories:

---

[3] Creswell, Qualitative Inquiry, 235.

[4] Sherr, Huff, and Curran, "Student Perceptions." In this study they list "Please finish this sentence—A professor who integrates faith and learning would never..." as an example of one of their study questions.

| Mentoring: | Preparation: |
|---|---|
| - Intentional | - Prayer |
| - In Situ | - Study |
| | |
| Modeling: | Motivation: |
| - Decision Making | - Service |
| - Organic/Integrous IFL | - Worhip |
| - Prayer (Practices) | - Connectivity |
| - Study (Practices) | |

Additionally, there were some responses in which the setting or locale was unclear, mostly because the interviewees were speaking hypothetically. These responses fell into three clusters of meaning with seven categories:

**Mentoring:**
  - Intentional
  - In Situ

**Modeling:**
  - Valuing
  - Study (Practices)
  - Interpersonal

**Preparation:**
  - Study

When taken together, the overall clusters of meaning and categories that students mentioned as being part of the ideal IFL were:

| Mentoring: | Preparation: |
|---|---|
| - Intentional | - Prayer |
| - In Situ | - Study |
| | |
| Modeling: | Motivation: |
| - Decision Making | - Purpose |
| - Interpersonal | - Service |
| - Valuing | - Worship |
| - Organic/Integrous IFL | - Connectivity |
| - Prayer (Practices) | |
| - Study (Practices) | |

These five clusters and their thirteen categories are the pieces of the puzzle that create the overall picture of how the students in the study imagined the ideal, most effective form of IFL happening in their theatre classes and production work. But it is not yet a completely accurate picture. In the above list all items are equal; one cannot weigh Connectivity, for example, against *In Situ* Mentoring because it is not known how often they were referenced. Thus more data is required, specifically the number of students who referenced each of the above categories and clusters, as well as the number of total references that were made to a category. These numbers will be included in the format (3/5), where 3 is the number of students who had referenced a particular category, and 5 is the number of total references to that category in the classroom, production, and other environments:

| | |
|---|---|
| **Mentoring: (5/16)** | |
| - Intentional (3/3) | |
| - In Situ (5/5) | |
| | |
| **Modeling: (9/42)** | |
| - Decision Making (6/10) | - Interpersonal (2/3) |
| - Valuing (8/12) | - Organic/Integrous IFL (4/7) |
| - Prayer (Practices) (3/3) | - Study (Practices) (5/7) |
| - Preparation (9/26) | - Prayer (6/8) |
| - Study (8/8) | - Motivation (7/9) |
| - Purpose | - Service (3/3) |
| - Worship (3/3) | - Connectivity (3/4) |

This chart best represents the student data for how that population imagined the ideal IFL in their program.[5] It is important to remember that there were nine total student participants in this study, including alumni/ ae. Thus the "Preparation: Study" category, for example, contained material from eight of the nine students, and had eighteen total references among the data collected from the four questions that addressed ideal perspectives. As a cluster, Preparation was referenced by all nine student participants and had twenty-six identifiable data points in the interview responses to the questions addressing ideals, making it the second-most referenced category in the study.

From this data several interesting points come to light. First, there are a number of categories that are statistically weak. Interpersonal Modeling only had three references from two persons, meaning that even in this relatively small population of nine students it was not a major part of how students imagined their ideal IFL. Further, both references were from alumni/ae, hinting that it may have been part of the instruction from a former professor(s) that was influential in the students' own imagining. Intentional Mentoring, Modeling: Prayer, and each of the three Motivation categories (Purpose, Service, and Worship) only had three references from three participants, showing that, though each was a *part* of the student ideal, they were not important enough to warrant much attention. All of these were relatively evenly split among past and current students. Interestingly, Connectivity with others (which included overt references to connectivity with God) was also only a small part of the student ideal: only one-third of the students referenced it (two alumni/ae and one current student), and only one of them mentioned it more than once. Also, even though it was a large part of the overall conversation with participants, as related to the *ideal*, an Organic or Integrous expression of IFL was mentioned by only four of the nine students, and repeated in the answers of only two. Additionally, though it was expected that Mentoring would be an important part of how students thought about faith integration, it was only mentioned six times (though by five different participants). This may be due to the

---

[5] For more detailed information regarding which participants referenced certain categories, readers may contact the author.

timeintensive nature of mentoring: only certain students could have the attention of a limited number of faculty. But the relatively small number of references to mentoring by the students is still noteworthy. Finally, Modeling: Study was referenced nearly exclusively by alumni/ae (there was only one reference by one current student). This may be interpreted several ways: (1) the modeling of this practice was understood to be valuable by students after they had graduated and had time to reflect on their experiences as a college student; (2) more modeling of study was done in years past but has since been done less frequently by the faculty; (3) or it is seen as less effective by the current students than by their predecessors. It is unclear from the data which interpretation is correct, and unfortunately one can only speculate on this point.

If the above points are interesting because they show low engagement by the students, there are several areas where students spoke effusively about their ideal integration of faith and learning. The expressions of ideal integration were most focused on the clusters Modeling and Preparation. Every student referenced some kind of modeling and some kind of preparatory practice as an essential part of the ideal faith integration. Specifically, Modeling: Valuing and Preparation: Study were identified by eight of the nine participants, twelve and eighteen times, respectively. Valuing was understood to be particularly important because it emphasized a part of the theatrical learning process that the majority of students referenced in their interviews: empathic understanding of another. By having faculty demonstrate the value of students through their actions (e.g., listening, caring, and treating them with respect), it made many of the students feel safe and loved, which was understood by the students to be part of the way Christian faith was expressed and integrated into the work of the faculty. Further, the preparatory practice of study was understood to be important because it provided opportunities for students to discover new facets of their faith as it related to their craft. As explained in chapter three, study in this instance referred to any type of exercise or assignment that provided a space for students to learn more about their craft and their faith simultaneously. This included everything from group discussion (S4), to faculty instruction about the spiritual side of character development, to classroom assignments like "shadow[ing] someone in their desired field who is living out a Christian worldview and writ[ing] a reflection paper on it" (A2). Thus, while it comes as no real surprise that student engagement with study was often spoken about, it can be encouraging for faculty to note that their efforts seem to be paying off, and that whether through predetermined assignments or through the rehearsal process, study was an invaluable part of the ideal integration process for students.

Continuing this examination of the data, six of the students mentioned prayer as being an important part of the ideal IFL, particularly in a production setting (where seven of the eight references took place). Interestingly, the current students seemed to find this more important than the alumni/ae (five references to three), but just barely. This implies that prayer was and continues to be an important part of how students desire faith integration to be enacted in their work. Finally, even though it was not mentioned as frequently as Modeling or Preparation, Motivation as a cluster also appears to be important, since some element of it was mentioned by seven of the nine students. Though there was division regarding what the motivation was (i.e., IFL provided purpose for their craft, it was a way of serving God and others, or it was a form of worship to God), all but one alumni/ae and one current student thought that having a motivation to pursue IFL was a necessary part of the ideal integration process. All told, however, even though Motivation and Preparation were important and vital parts of the ideal student IFL, the forty-two times that some form of Modeling was mentioned in response to the four questions clearly indicates that the intentional faculty presentation of faith integration through modeling was *essential* for how students imagined IFL occurring. The role of faculty not just as purveyors of knowledge but as the personified representation of faith in action speaks to the level of influence that these theatre students have placed upon faculty shoulders.

**Faculty IFL Ideals**

The faculty population within this study had a much broader understanding of faith integration than did their student counterparts, as evidenced in the wide variety of ways that they talked about its manifestation. In just speaking about their ideal imaginings of IFL, faculty mentioned all six of the clusters of meaning that were identified in chapter four. Further, within those six clusters fully twenty of the twenty-two categories that were discovered were also mentioned.

For the classroom setting, five clusters and fifteen categories were mentioned by the faculty:

| **Instruction:** | **Identity:** |
|---|---|
| - Engaged | - Self-Awareness |
| - Self-Discovery | |
| - Lecture | **Preparation:** |
| - Discussion | - Study |
| - Organic IFL | |
| - Structured IFL | **Motivation:** |
| | - Faith Preparation |
| **Modeling:** | - Connectivity to others |
| - Prayer | - Purpose |
| - Interpersonal | |
| - Study | |
| - Organic IFL | |

For the production setting, all six clusters and seventeen categories were part of the faculty ideal IFL:

| Instruction: | Mentoring: |
|---|---|
| - Self-Discovery | - Intentional |
| - Discussion | - In Situ |
| - Lecture | |
| - Organic IFL | Preparation: |
| - Structured IFL | - Prayer |
| | - Study |
| Modeling: | |
| - Prayer | Motivation: |
| -Study | - Evangelism |
| | - Faith Preparation |
| Identity: | - Connectivity to God/others |
| -Self-Awareness | - Professional Training |

Further, as with the student data there were some responses in which the setting or locale was unclear, or where the setting was clearly not a classroom or a production (e.g., meeting over a meal). These responses fell into five clusters of meaning with ten categories:

| | Mentoring: |
|---|---|
| Instruction: | - Intentional |
| - Organic IFL | - In Situ |
| | |
| Modeling: | Motivation: |
| - Interpersonal | - Evangelism |
| | - Faith Preparation |
| - Organic/Integrous IFL | - Connectivity to others |
| | - Professional Training |
| Identity: | |
| - Self Awareness | |

101

When *combined*, the larger aggregate list of six clusters and twenty categories becomes:

| Instruction: | Mentoring: |
|---|---|
| - Engaged | - Intentional |
| - Self-Discovery | - In Situ |
| - Lecture | |
| - Discussion | Preparation: |
| - Organic IFL | - Prayer |
| - Structured IFL | - Study |
| | |
| Modeling: | Motivation: |
| - Prayer | - Evangelism |
| - Interpersonal | - Faith Preparation |
| - Study  Organic IFL | - Connectivity to God/others |
| | - Professional Training |
| Identity: | - Purpose |
| - Self-Awareness | |

Finally, let us include the number of faculty who referenced each of the above categories and clusters, as well as the number of total references that were made to a category. These numbers will be illustrated in the same way as in the student data above. It should be remembered there were a total of six faculty members interviewed for this study (the number of full-time faculty who teach theatre students in the theatre department).

| Instruction: (6/31) | Identity: (2/4) |
|---|---|
| - Engaged (2/5) | - Self-Awareness (2/4) |
| - Self-Discovery (3/4) | |
| - Lecture (2/2) | Mentoring: (4/10) |
| Discussion (3/5) | - Intentional (3/5) |
| - Organic IFL (5/13) | - In Situ (3/5) |
| - Structured IFL (2/2) | |
| | Preparation: (4/7) |
| Modeling: (6/13) | - Prayer (1/1) |
| - Prayer (3/3) | - Study (4/6) |
| - Interpersonal (3/4) | |
| - Study (2/3) | Motivation: (6/25) |
| - Organic IFL (3/3) | - Evangelism (3/4) |
| | - Faith Preparation (4/6) |
| | - Professional Training (3/4) |
| | - Purpose (1/2) |
| | - Connectivity to God/others (4/6) |

This data best represent the responses given by the faculty to questions that sought to discover how they imagined the ideal IFL happening within their department.

From this data a few observations arise. First, the diversity of ways that the faculty understood the ideal faith integration is telling. As supported by various statements elsewhere in their interviews, the faculty largely saw their efforts as one part of a larger departmental and university-wide push for faith integration.

Consequently, in their ideal there would not be one uniform way of approaching faith integration, but rather it would manifest in diversity, where a wide variety of pedagogical methods might be employed so that every student (and every learning style) might find resonance. Second, unlike with the student ideals, no single cluster or even category jumps out from the others as being of greater importance. Whereas with the students there were two clusters that appeared in all nine interviews, with the faculty there are three (Instruction, Modeling, and Motivation), and two more were mentioned by a majority (Mentoring and Preparation). This seems to further support their desire for diverse IFL engagement. But while this point holds true, there are a few particular categories and clusters that deserve additional attention here.

The first is Instruction. Though not the only cluster to be spoken of by all six of the faculty, it had the largest number of references (thirty-one) within the various responses to the four questions. Specifically, an Organic or Integrous expression of IFL was the most-referenced type of instruction, with five of the six faculty referring to it a total of thirteen times. Interestingly enough the majority of the references (ten of thirteen) came from a classroom setting (as opposed to the stage, where it would be more expected within the production process). Thus it seems that the faculty imagine their greatest influence or ability to share their faith comes from the organic expression of it within the material that they are teaching in traditional educational settings. This expression, though organic and natural in presentation, would derive from other pedagogical approaches, such as discussion, student self-discovery, and even (paradoxically) structured lectures and moments where the subject of faith was intentionally brought to the forefront of a lesson plan. And for nearly all of the faculty, Organic/Integrous IFL would ideally arise because of their natural inclination to live in a Christ-like way while teaching their subject. As F3 stated, "There is so much spiritual about what we do, I have to keep myself from talking about it in order to get other stuff taught."

The second cluster that was mentioned by all faculty as part of their ideal IFL was Motivation (6/25). Whether it was to provide professional training, to prepare students to actively engage with their Christian faith, or to prepare students to share their faith in and during their professional careers, all faculty shared that their motivation was what led to the ideal IFL becoming a reality. This seems to imply that faculty could not just "do" faith integration as an "add-on" assignment; it had to have a purpose and reason for being part of their particular curriculum. Further, for most of the faculty that purpose was multifaceted: professional training was important because it would allow students to be taken seriously, which then would allow them to share their faith with colleagues; or, relatedly, as part of professional training students would be encouraged to actively seek after spiritual maturity so that they could connect with God or with colleagues in ways that would allow for spiritual matters to arise when they entered into the industry. In either interpretation, however, it was clear from at least five of the six faculty that spiritual and professional preparation went hand in hand with their instruction.

The third cluster referenced by all the faculty was Modeling. However, although Modeling was the overwhelming favorite of the student groups, it was clearly less important than Motivation and Instruction for the faculty: it was referenced only thirteen times (compared to forty-two times by students), and its most referenced category (Interpersonal) only had four data points among the interviews. Even so, faculty did seem to at least acknowledge that their position naturally made them role models for faith integration, and that modeling occurred in all settings. In fact, of the thirteen references, five were in the classroom, four were in production environments, and four were in other locales, making it the most evenly split cluster of any of those mentioned.

One final point to mention here is that even though only four of the six faculty mentioned Mentoring as part of their ideal IFL, as a group they still believed it to be more important than the student population did: two-thirds of the faculty mentioned it a total of ten times, whereas five of the nine students mentioned it a total of six times. In particular, Intentional Mentoring was given greater attention by the faculty, though it was acknowledged to be difficult to manage with the other duties expected of them as collegiate professors. As one professor put it, "I consider myself to be tied together [with my students] as a mentor for their life. I mean, obviously I'm not going to see them as much as I do when they're here, but I want to know... how they're doing five or ten years down the road. I think that's what's unique about being at a Christian university."

**Ideal Connections, Divergences, and Essences**

As stated above, there were differences in the numbers between student and faculty responses to both Modeling and Mentoring: students clearly favored Modeling in their ideal IFL scenarios, and faculty thought Mentoring was a bit more important than the students did. But there are other similarities and differences that warrant a few lines of text.

First, though obvious, it is important to note that the faculty devoted much of their answers to their instruction, particularly the pedagogical approaches used to bring about IFL. While students did speak about their professors' faith and professional knowledge, it was primarily through how they modeled that knowledge, not through how it was presented, that was important. Thus each group placed a different emphasis on how knowledge was conveyed. Second, though it is a small point, two of the six faculty members stated that their understandings of self were part of their ideal IFL. For F1, this related to how she viewed herself in relation to God: she modeled her work after how God worked, and her understanding of her Christian faith, which was "central to everything we do," affected her worldview and her approach to teaching and creating art. F5 understood that her faith "should somehow inform the art that I create in some shape, form, or fashion," and that she was created to be an artist who is a Christian. Interestingly, however, she also freely acknowledged that even with all her experience she was unable to provide all answers to all questions posed by students, even though her years of teaching had "settled" her understanding of faith and art in relation to each other. This freedom to not know, combined with her self-identity as a Christ-follower who engages her artistic talents, formed a truthful persona that informed the way she approached her craft as an educator, and further shaped her approach to IFL. It is worth noting that both of these faculty believed that their selfawareness was critical to their profession. Further, it can be surmised that they believed their self-awareness to be evident to their students; that the students could see their faith, their understanding of God, and their sense of purpose through their ideal teaching. The truthfulness of this assumption seems to be affirmed in the responses of the students: since nearly half of all the cluster references from the student groups were related to some kind of Modeling, it does in fact appear that students placed great value on the way faculty lived out their faith through their practices and interactions, and that it was evident to them. Or, it should be clarified, that it would *ideally* be evident to them (as these responses only address ideals, not necessarily actuality).

Third, both groups placed a relatively equal value on Motivation. While neither group saw it as the most important part of their ideal IFL, both widely acknowledged that it was a critical part of their faith integration: seven of nine students and all six faculty referenced it. While motivations differed (e.g., S4 was motivated by understanding human emotion, whereas F1 was motivated by sending out professionally trained evangelists [the author's term]), nearly everyone believed that having a purpose for doing IFL was necessary. Finally, though it was stated above, it is worth repeating that the faculty had a much broader perspective on how faith integration should ideally happen. Even with only six participants, they identified six different models of ideal instruction, both types of mentoring, both types of preparation, and five different types of motivation (compared to three types by the student groups). They also added an entirely new cluster, Identity. Only Modeling had more student categories (six were identified by the students, compared to four by the faculty). Thus it can be extrapolated that their understanding of the ideal integration of faith and learning was more complex and varied than that of their students, which supported their desires to let it be part of their organic teaching styles.

So how then, with this foundation underfoot, can we describe what both students and faculty imagine to be the ideal integration of faith and learning, and how do they imagine it? Or put another way, how might it be textually and structurally described? Further, what is the essence, the "essential invariant structure" of their experiences? Let us start with the student populations.

For the students, they imagine the ideal integration of faith and learning to be connection-oriented. These connections are formed foremost through the models they have in their instructors, through trusting mentoring relationships, and through how they prepare for their callings as artists of faith. Many are motivated to cultivate connections by using their art to serve others, to worship God, or to provide a larger sense of purpose for their lives. They prepare not only by studying their craft but also through prayer and studying their faith in relation to their craft. This preparation provides connectivity with their instructors, with each other, and with God. *Therefore, the essence of what was imagined and how it was imagined was that a deep-seated, spiritual, and tri-directional connectivity between students, faculty, and God would occur through professional and personal relationship building, brought about through shared motivations, right preparation, and trust-based relationships where mentoring and modeling could occur.*

For the faculty, they imagined the ideal integration of faith and learning to happen largely in an organic way through their instructional practices. These practices illuminated the various motivations that drove the faculty to teach theatre

105

in a Christian environment, motivations that sought to balance out the professional training of students and preparation to be faithful Christ-followers in the entertainment industry. Because of the nature of theatrical learning, instructional practices often involved both modeling and mentoring, including the sharing of both professional knowledge and spiritual insights that come with experience and maturity. *Thus, the essence of what was imagined regarding the ideal faith integration and how it was imagined was that it was an organic process brought about through a desire to strike a proper balance between professional instruction and faith-based preparation for students to work in the entertainment industry. This organic process would occur through varied pedagogies, including both mentoring and modeling, and had the goal of creating a lasting connection between students, their profession, and God.*

**Student IFL Perceptions**

Just as students were asked four questions that dealt with their imagined ideal for integration of faith and learning, they were also asked six questions that attempted to uncover their general perceptions of actual faith integration:

(1) *Do you believe faith integration is beneficial to your field or craft? If yes, how so?*

(2) *Describe an example of faith integration occurring in a class you've taken for your major. What other examples can you offer?*

(3) *Describe an example of faith integration occurring in a production that you've been a part of. What other examples can you offer?*

(4) *Using a scale of 1 to 10, I want you to select and rank three professors based on your perceptions of their efforts to integrate faith and learning in the classroom. Without using their names or any identifying information, please describe how you arrived at the value for each professor.*

(5) *How have you changed spiritually during your time here at [blank]? Do you think your experience as a Theatre student has had any impact on that change? Can you give an example?*

(6) *Do you think your professors within your department are interested or concerned with your faith? If yes, how do you know?*

As with the questions that sought to discover student ideal imaginings, these questions were developed to better engage the two distinct learning environments where students and faculty regularly interact within the department (the classroom and the stage), and also to maintain some continuity with the Sherr, Huff, and Curran study from 2007, mentioned above. For example, the fourth question in this list was taken straight from their study, in order to compare results. The first question was asked in order to determine their general sense and understanding of faith integration in their department. The fifth question was included in order to get students to reflect not just on the assignments or projects that were oriented toward faith integration (such as might appear in the answers to questions 2 and 3), but to get them to reflect on the significance and result of those assignments and other influencers that came to the fore during their interviews. The last question was asked to provide students with an opportunity to move away from texts, assignments, and projects and think instead about the ways faculty interacted with them; it provided a way to compare how students perceived their faculty with how the faculty perceived themselves.

Among the students that were interviewed, five different clusters of meaning were identified as illustrative of how students perceived IFL in a classroom setting, and within those five clusters there were a total of twelve categories:

| | |
|---|---|
| **Mentoring:**<br>   -In Situ<br><br>**Modeling:**<br>   -Decision Making<br>   -Interpersonal<br>   -Valuing<br>   -Organic/Integrous IFL<br>   -Prayer (Practices)<br>   -Study (Practices) | **Preparation:**<br>   -Prayer<br>   -Study<br><br>**Motivation:**<br>   -Purpose<br>   -Service<br>   -Connectivity to others |

Similarly, within the production settings, students illuminated five clusters of meaning with thirteen categories:

| | |
|---|---|
| **Mentoring:**<br>   - Intentional<br>   - In Situ<br><br>**Modeling:**<br>   - Decision Making<br>   - Interpersonal<br>   - Valuing<br>   - Organic/Integrous IFL<br>   - Prayer (Practices)<br>   - Study (Practices) | **Preparation:**<br>   - Prayer<br>   - Study<br><br>**Motivation:**<br>   - Purpose<br>   - Service<br>   - Connectivity to others |

Further, as in the data sets that examined student ideals there were some responses in which the setting or locale was unclear. These responses fell into all five clusters of meaning with eleven categories:

| Mentoring: | Preparation: |
|---|---|
| - Intentional | - Study |
| - In Situ | |
| | Motivation: |
| Modeling: | - Purpose |
| - Interpersonal | - Service |
| - Valuing | - Connectivity with others |
| - Organic/Integrous IFL | |
| - Prayer (Practices) | |
| - Study (Practices) | |

When taken together, the overall clusters of meaning and categories that students mentioned as being part of their perceived IFL were:

| Mentoring: | Preparation: |
|---|---|
| - Intentional | - Prayer |
| - In Situ | - Study |
| | |
| Modeling: | Motivation: |
| - Decision Making | - Purpose |
| - Interpersonal | - Service |
| - Valuing | - Connectivity to others |
| - Organic/Integrous IFL | |
| - Prayer (Practices) | |
| - Study (Practices) | |

These five clusters and their thirteen categories represent student perceptions of actual IFL efforts within their department. But just as it was necessary to include data that allowed for the comparison of categories and clusters within the section on student ideals, so too is it necessary here. Now let us plug in the number of students who referenced each of the above categories and clusters, as well as the number of total references that were made to a category:

| Mentoring: (9/23) | Preparation: (9/23) |
|---|---|
| - Intentional (4/7) | - Prayer (4/4) |
| - In Situ (9/16) | - Study (9/19) |
| | |
| Modeling: (9/97) | Motivation: (9/26) |
| - Decision Making (4/7) | - Purpose (8/16) |
| - Interpersonal (6/13) | - Service (5/10) |
| - Valuing (9/25) | - Connectivity (9/23) |
| - Organic/Integrous IFL (9/20) | |
| - Prayer (Practices) (6/12) | |
| - Study (Practices) (8/20) | |

This chart best represents the student data regarding how that population perceived IFL in their program.[6]

Several interesting observations may be made regarding the data for student perceptions. First, unlike the data presented regarding student (or faculty) ideals, every student referenced each of the five clusters during their interviews. While this can partly be explained by having more questions to answer (six questions dealt with perceptions, whereas only four dealt with ideals), it also speaks to the common threads that held the interviews together and the apparent interpretive validity of the data. Second, just as Modeling was the dominant cluster in the ideal data sets, so too was it the dominant data set within student perceptions, by far. Indeed, it was referenced nearly four times as often as the next closest cluster, Motivation (ninety-seven times for Modeling, twenty-six times for Motivation). This confirms what was presented earlier: students were far more conscientious of faculty modeling regarding IFL than any other medium of dissemination. Further, given that over half of the student population in this study were graduates from the department and had had several years to either retain or forget collegiate experiences, the data also implies that the Modeling experiences referenced were also some of the most influential in how the alumni/ae came to understand their own faith. As S3 said, "The people that I'm going to remember most in ten years are the professors and the staff and the people who modeled what I want to be in the future.... I'm looking to my professors and my directors as an example."

Building off of the last point, while Modeling increased the most dramatically, three of the four other clusters also all significantly increased when asked about perceptions as opposed to ideals: Mentoring rose from 5/6 to 9/23; Motivation rose from 7/9 to 9/26; and Connectivity rose from 3/4 to 9/23. Only Preparation remained largely unchanged (9/26 for ideals, and 9/23 for perceptions). This may partly be explained by the increase in questions that were asked, allowing students more opportunities to speak about these categories. But that cannot be the sole explanation, as one would expect to find only a 50 percent increase in response data points (correlating with the 50 percent increase in questions asked), whereas in actuality the increases are far more substantial: 283 percent for Mentoring, 189 percent for Motivation, and a whopping 675 percent for Connectivity. So why the increases? The author suspects that it has to do with the types of questions asked: many of them allowed the interviewees to provide multiple examples, and one question specifically sought IFL data for how students perceived three different faculty members. Thus their answers were longer and more diverse, and consequently gave more data points to discover and code. But regardless of the cause it is clear that all of these five clusters are an essential part of how students perceived IFL within their department.

It is also striking that with the exception of Modeling, the four other clusters are all nearly equal with regard to the number of times they were referenced by the student populations, and three of the four clusters are exactly that (9/23, 9/23,

---

[6] For more detailed information regarding which participants referenced certain categories, please contact the author.

9/26, and 9/23). It is therefore impossible to say that, between these four, one is more statistically significant than the other.[7] Rather, each played an important part in the perceptions of the nine student participants. While it may be a stretch to say that each cluster holds equal meaning to the students (these are, after all, *perceptions*, not value statements), their presence in all nine interviews cannot be ignored. Further, in the large majority of instances these data points arose out of positive examples, instances where a faculty member or peer did something that was deemed by the student to be a good representation of IFL. Consequently it can be reasonably inferred that while Modeling was far and away the most cited (and likely influential) type of IFL, each of the five clusters represent essential ways that many students perceive, interpret, and benefit from faith integration. Each cluster should thus be considered by the faculty when designing faith integration models for the department (more about this will be said in chapter six).

Before moving on to summarize faculty perceptions of IFL, we must pause here briefly to address the question that first fertilized the soil from which this study eventually sprouted: would the responses of theatre students in this study be consistent with the responses given by students of various fields of study in the research done by Sherr, Huff, and Curran? Now that we have examined all of the student data, the answer can be brought to light. In their findings Sherr, Huff, and Curran stated that "student perceptions of IFL indicators fall into two main categories—faculty relationships and faculty competence." The "faculty relationships" refer to the faculty's relationships with God, and "the breadth and depth expected of these relationships," as well as their relationships with students.[8] "Faculty competence" referred to an aptitude with any kind of IFL "curriculum," even if it was primarily through the sharing of IFL experiences, and a competency with creating a classroom environment where "a group culture that elicits feelings of belonging, acceptance, and commitment [exists]." This competence was largely seen as effective when the faculty members' efforts at IFL "appeared natural and authentic" instead of forced or uncomfortable.[9]

In comparing this study to that done by Sherr, Huff, and Curran it is clear that there are points of commonality. Though the data have been explained differently, faculty Modeling was the largest cluster in both student ideals and student perceptions, and captures much of what the previous study describes as "relationship" and "competence": faculty Decision Making largely encompasses how a faculty member chooses to talk about God, what they choose to teach, and how they handle conflict or uncomfortable situations with students and others, which in turn reflects the way they think about God and what kinds of relationships they have with their students; both the Interpersonal and Valuing categories were ways to capture how students felt that their faculty cared for them personally, both

---

[7] Though Motivation technically has three more data points than the other clusters, it is hard to say that it is therefore more signifi-cant. For example, seven of those twenty-six references all come from one participant, A4. Thus, while perhaps Motivation was very important for her, it skews the data enough that it becomes difficult to state definitively that it should be ranked as more significant than the others.

[8] Sherr, Huff and Curran, "Student Perceptions," 21.

[9] Sherr, Huff and Curran, "Student Perceptions," 24.

within and beyond the classroom, which paralleled the desire for faculty competence in creating a safe environment; the practices of Prayer and Study were understood to be demonstrations of the faculty's relationship with God and their competence with their curriculum, respectively; and the Organic/Integrous IFL category of Modeling represented the ways in which students most appreciated, remembered, or idealized IFL happening, which mirrors the "natural" approach students preferred in the Sherr, Huff, and Curran study. Thus the Modeling cluster alone supports the findings in the original study. But this new research also hints that theatre students, or at least *these* theatre students, perceived more than those who interacted with their faculty primarily in the classroom, as those in the 2007 study appear to have done. The nine theatre students also spoke about their own roles in faith integration, such as the need for proper preparatory practices like prayer and study (including rehearsals, character research, historical study, design work, vocal training, and even Biblical study), as well as their own motivations that were driven by a desire to serve or to pursue a dream because of a larger, faith-driven purpose. They also felt that they were more connected with their faculty because of the many and varied opportunities to interact with them in class, in rehearsal, building sets, and in planned or spontaneous meetings. Thus while the Sherr, Huff, and Curran findings hold true for the nine representative theatre majors, they do not capture everything; the actual perceptions of IFL within their department were far more nuanced and diverse than those of a general student population.

**Faculty IFL Perceptions**

Faculty were asked five questions that sought to address their perceptions of IFL within their department. For all intents and purposes they were the same questions that were asked of the students, minus the question asking that they rank three professors on their IFL efforts:

(1) *Do you believe faith integration is beneficial to your field or craft? If yes, how so?*

(2) *Describe an example of faith integration occurring in a class you've taught for the Theatre Department. What other examples can you offer?*

(3) *Describe an example of faith integration occurring in a production that you've been a part of. What other examples can you offer?*

(4) *How have you changed spiritually during your time here at [blank]? Do you think your experience as a Theatre faculty member has had any impact on that change?*

(5) *Do you think your fellow professors within the department are interested in or concerned with your faith? If yes, how do you know?*

As with faculty ideals, all six clusters of meaning that were identified in chapter four were found in the faculty perceptions as well. And, just as with the ideals, within those six clusters twenty of the twenty-two categories that were discovered were mentioned.

For the classroom setting four of the six clusters and thirteen categories were mentioned by the faculty.

| **Instruction:** | **Mentoring:** |
|---|---|
| - Engaged | - In Situ |
| - Self-Discovery | |
| - Lecture | **Preparation:** |
| - Discussion | - Study |
| - Organic/Integrous IFL | - Motivation |
| - Evangelism | - Professional Training |
| - Faith Preparation | - Purpose |
| - Connectivity to others | |
| - Structured IFL | |

For the production setting, all six clusters but only twelve categories were part of the faculty perceptions of IFL:

| **Instruction:** | **Mentoring:** |
|---|---|
| - Self-Discovery | - In Situ |
| - Discussion | |
| - Organic/Integrous IFL | **Preparation:** |
| -   Structured IFL | - Study |
| | |
| **Modeling:** | **Motivation:** |
| - Study | - Evangelism |
| - Organic/Integrous IFL | - Connectivity to God/others |
| | - Professional Training |
| **Identity:** | |
| - Self-Awareness | |

For the data where the locale or setting was not clear, or where it was not in a classroom or a production environment, the responses spanned all six clusters of meaning with fifteen categories, making this the largest of the three possible settings, and the one with the greatest number of individual data points:

| **Instruction:** | **Preparation:** |
|---|---|
| - Engaged | - Prayer |
| - Discussion | - Accountability |
| | - Study |
| **Modeling:** | |
| - Interpersonal | **Motivation:** |
| - Study | - Evangelism |
| - Organic/Integrous IFL | - Faith Preparation |
| | - Connectivity with others |
| **Identity:** | - Professional Training |
| - Self-Awareness | - Purpose |
| | |
| **Mentoring:** | |
| - Intentional | |

112

When combined, the larger aggregate list of six clusters and twenty categories becomes:

| Instruction: | Preparation: |
|---|---|
| - Engaged | - Prayer |
| - Self-Discovery | - Accountability |
| - Structured IFL | - Study |
| | |
| **Modeling:** | **Motivation:** |
| - Interpersonal | - Evangelism |
| - Study | - Faith Preparation |
| - Organic/Integrous IFL | - Connectivity to God/others |
| | - Professional Training |
| **Identity:** | - Purpose |
| - Self-Awareness | |
| | |
| **Mentoring:** | |
| - Intentional | |
| - In Situ | |
| - Lecture | |
| - Discussion | |
| - Organic/Integrous IFL | |

And one last time, the number of faculty who referenced each of the above categories and clusters, as well as the number of total references that were made to a category need to be included in order to allow for data comparisons:

| Instruction: (6/32) | Mentoring: (2/3) |
|---|---|
| - Engaged (6/8) | - Intentional (1/1) |
| - Self-Discovery (5/8) | - In Situ (2/2) |
| - Lecture (1/1) | |
| - Discussion (3/6) | **Preparation: (5/12)** |
| - Organic/Integrous IFL (3/4) | - Prayer (1/1) |
| - Structured IFL (4/5) | - Accountability (2/2) |
| | - Study (4/9) |
| **Modeling: (4/10)** | |
| - Interpersonal (2/2) | **Motivation: (6/55)** |
| - Study (3/4) | - Evangelism (5/15) |
| - Organic/Integrous IFL (3/4) | - Faith Preparation (6/11) |
| | - Professional Training (5/10) |
| **Identity:** | - Purpose (3/3) |
| - Self-Awareness (5/7) | - Connectivity to God/others (6/16) |

This data best represents the responses given by the faculty to questions that sought to discover how they perceived actual IFL happening within their department.

As with previous data, this information leads to a few observations. First, it is surprising to note that faculty had nothing to say about their perceived modeling in the classroom. Though this will be expanded upon in the next section, it is mystifying that a cluster with so much significance to the student population should get so little attention from the faculty. Rather, of the thirteen categories referenced by the faculty within the classroom setting, Instruction constituted six categories and Motivation constituted five. This clearly shows that the faculty viewed their pedagogical approaches to faith integration, and their personal motivations for integrating faith in their subjects, as the most important factors in how they perceive IFL.

Second, whereas all the clusters in the student responses reflected the entirety of the population interviewed, only two of the clusters were addressed by the entire faculty population: Instruction and Motivation. Motivation had the overwhelming majority of references (fifty-five) within the interviews, but Instruction was not too far behind (thirty-two), and, taken together, these numbers seem to imply that faculty believed their *purposes* for integrating faith and learning would communicate in the way they presented their material. Or put another way, it was believed that their motivation (e.g., to prepare students to share their faith in the industry) shaped the way they communicated their subject matter (e.g., through structured assignments or self-discovery exercises). While this was likely true,[10] it nonetheless does not leave much room for the other clusters of importance, or for the varied ways that students seemed to perceive IFL most acutely. Interestingly, Organic/Integrous IFL, which was overwhelmingly stated by the faculty to be the most ideal type of IFL instruction, was not very present in the way faculty perceived their own efforts at teaching IFL. While this may simply be the result of humility, one would expect to find more alignment with faculty ideals and perceptions since they have the greatest ability to adapt or change their instructional methods.

Finally, because Motivation and Instruction were the top data clusters by far, the other four clusters lagged significantly behind. After Motivation (6/55) and Instruction (6/32) the numbers drop: Preparation (5/12), Modeling (4/10), Identity (specifically Self-Awareness, 5/7), and Mentoring (2/3) all statistically underwhelm. Faculty preparation was a more conscious component of how they perceived IFL than it was in their ideals, especially with regard to study (usually of their field, though also of faith integration), but this is to be expected since (a) there was an additional question to increase the possible data, and (b) the author has yet to meet a professor who dreams (idealizes) about doing more class prep. The numbers for Modeling and Mentoring perceptions both decreased compared to their ideal counterparts. With no references to Modeling within the classroom this comes as no surprise, but it again runs counter to student perceptions and ideals, and even to faculty ideals. And though it is merely educated speculation, Mentoring likely decreased because of the constraints on faculty time: several faculty spoke at length about time pressures (both external and internal to the department) that kept them from engaging in personal conversations with each other about faith, for example, and that likely translated to their ability to have these same kinds of conversations with students as well. As the data shows, whereas four faculty envisioned Mentoring as part of their ideal IFL, only two actually perceived it happening.

---

[10] Indeed, many of this author's own pedagogical choices in the classroom arise out of his own convictions, his own understanding of what he hopes students will do with the knowledge that is imparted to them, and the type of information that he hopes they will gain from the course.

## Perception Connections, Divergences, and Essences

The ways that students perceived faith integration in their department had few points of commonality, and many points of departure, from those of their faculty. With respect to the points where the two populations found shared agreement, the most obvious was in the types of categories that arose during the interviews. Both populations spoke about many of the same kinds of Modeling, the same kinds of Mentoring, and the same kinds of Preparation for perceived effective IFL. Both groups also spoke of how the field of theatre lends itself to the creation of "connections" between students, between faculty and students, and between each group and God. These connections found expression through the types of instruction, modeling, mentoring, and training that happened during the academic year, and were largely seen as necessary for effective IFL to happen. However, even though both groups placed great value on their connections, they seemed at times to be speaking of their perceptions of IFL in completely different ways.

To begin, it was startling to discover that, while students placed incredible weight on the role of faculty as models for effective perceived IFL (9/97), the faculty themselves made absolutely *no* mention of Modeling in their statements about the classroom, and only a relative handful of references to it in productions or nonspecified locations (4/10). Indeed, fully one third of the faculty made no mention of it at all! While faculty saw it as a small but important part of the *ideal* integration of faith and learning, they either downplayed their own roles as models in real life so much that Modeling became nearly nonexistent, or they actually had little to no perception of the role-model status of their profession. This trend continues, not unexpectedly, in Mentoring, which was the smallest of any faculty cluster: whereas every student said mentoring was an important part of how they perceived faith integration (9/23), the faculty only gave it a cursory nod (2/3). The faculty, again not unexpectedly, devoted far more time to the types of Instruction that were a part of their pedagogical repertoire; in the faculty data, three of the six Instruction categories had at least twice as many references as all of Mentoring combined. The students, however, *did not even have an Instruction cluster.* For them, as for the students in the Sherr, Huff, and Curran study, the type of educational atmosphere that a professor created, an atmosphere that included effective modeling of faith integration, was far more memorable (and thus likely more effective) than any particular technique. Specifically, did the professor create an atmosphere where the students felt valued, listened to, and a part of the learning process? When they did so, the students believed it demonstrated a living out of their faith. Two examples of this come from S1 and S3. From S1, "I make it a point to listen to my professors, because I do think that they're intelligent and that they do have something to say. But if I don't agree with them—I will never disrespect them, but I should be able to say, 'I don't agree.' And then, 'Help me to understand what you're saying if I don't understand, and if I do understand but don't agree, then I just don't agree.'" Thus S1 wanted to be heard, and wanted to be allowed to engage in the learning process. For S3, this extended even further:

> If you have a professor who is clearly teaching from a very secular mindset and then all of a sudden faith integration comes up like midway through the semester and they're like, "Oh yeah, so you have to do this faith integration thing, meh, I guess we'll write some papers about Jesus

and then we'll get on with our lives." Then it's like, it's pretty clear that they don't really... see it as a necessary component of a course. And so I think the way you treat faith integration is really important too, as a professor. Because you can tell very clearly how a professor feels [about] the faith integration component of... coursework by the way that they introduce it and the way they talk about it.

She then went on to speak about a professor who *did* care about faith integration.

But the way that he treats them is very respecting and very God fearing and very... not somberly, not like it's this depressing horrible thing that we have to talk about in class and go over and write papers on, but he just treats it very like, respectfully and very—he honors the fact that although it has nothing to do with [class content] it's a very important thing that we should be doing. And he even said in class, like, "Does this have anything to do with [class content]? No. That being said, does it have anything to do with your betterment as a faith-centered individual later on in life? Yes. We're going to do it." And I was like, okay, here we go.

Thus, generally speaking, the way a professor chose to engage with faith integration, communicate the value of it to their students, and demonstrate the value of it through their own behaviors and actions influenced the way that the students engaged with IFL efforts.

In addition to the lack of faculty attention to Modeling and Mentoring, and the lack of student attention to Instruction, another area of divergence between student and faculty responses was the subject of where IFL happened. This location was not so much a physical location, however, as a direction of focus. For the faculty, IFL clusters largely dealt with self: their own Motivations, Preparation, understandings of Identity, and pedagogies. For the students, it was more directed at others: others who mentored, others who modeled, and others to connect with. While self-motivation and self-preparation were certainly important factors, fully three of the five clusters and 143 of the 192 data-point references (74.4 percent) within the various categories were directed outwards. This is not surprising since (a) students come to the university to learn from others, (b) faculty have had more time than students to develop and explore their own faith, and (c) faith-based instruction often requires a knowledge of one's own faith in greater detail in order to be able to answer questions intelligently. But it once again shows that the two groups do not quite seem to be talking on the same frequency; the data from this study (albeit limited in scope) seems to imply that students are not aware of how faculty are trying to effectively integrate their faith into their teaching, and that faculty are perhaps too inwardly focused and missing opportunities (particularly Modeling opportunities) to illustrate how faith and theatre coexist in the lives of professionals.

There is one final point of divergence between the two groups' perceptions of IFL. and it relates to each group's Motivations. For the faculty, there were several motivating factors that compelled them to pursue faith integration (in addition to the fact that the university actively encouraged it). These factors converged into a desire to prepare students to be high-quality professionals, while at the same time preparing them both to continue maturing in their faith and to be confident living out and sharing their faith with others as appropriate. The students, however, seemed to have very different motivations, at least initially. Within the student Motivations cluster only two categories emerged: Purpose, which meant that students derived a sense of purpose from their lives as artists of faith; and Service, which meant that students were motivated to pursue theatre as a way to serve the various communities in which they resided. Among the Service respondents, however, four were alumni/ae and only one was a current student, making it appear that this Motivation possibly arose after leaving school and entering the "real world," or that it was connected with previous instructors or classes that are no longer offered. In any case, Purpose was the only Motivation that was consistent across both past and current students (four alumni/ae and four current students). The purposes (or the senses of purpose that IFL brought to theatrical studies) were diverse and wide-ranging, including: to bring "light to God" and God's creation (S3); to tell the stories "the right way" by telling them truthfully and hopefully "pointing to faith and grace" (S2); to deal with industry rejection (A4); to provide a "constant and reliable" place to stand as an actor instead of being caught up in fame and fortune; to "teach us to place our value in Christ" (A2); to learn how to bring "truth and life to a story," which mimics how Christ "brought truth and life into our story here on earth and gave us a purpose" (A1); and to help students to love and accept others because of exposure to different types of people (S4). While some of these purposes align with the faculty Motivations, others appear to miss the faculty's perceived intentions. Indeed, several of these student purposes seem to have more to do with story interpretation and self-care than with professional skill sets or the confident sharing of faith through action and speech. Thus, there seems to be a breakdown in communication of stated intentions between what drives the faculty and what the students see as the intended purpose of faith integration. Suggestions on how this might be addressed will be given in chapter six.

So how then, after all this, can we distill *what* was perceived by the students and faculty and *how* they perceived it? Or, stated another way, how can each group's perceptions be textually and structurally described? And, as this is a phenomenological study, what is the essence, the "essential, invariant structure," of what each perceived?

The students perceived the integration of faith and learning to be an amalgamation of external and internal influences that were directed toward a natural living out of their beliefs in and through theatrical practices. Of these influences, external modeling was the most significant and lasting, but the influences of mentors and the connections that students had with faculty, staff, and other peers, as well as the internal motivations and preparatory practices that propelled them to continue studying in the field, were also all equally a part of what students deemed to be effective faith integration. *Therefore, the essence of what students perceive to be effective integration of faith and learning is a supportive, networked web of methodologies, relationships, and practices, centered around professional and spiritual modeling, that foster a greater understanding of God and of humanity.*

The faculty perceived the integration of faith and learning to be motivated by their desire to prepare students for the professional and spiritual realities of the profession and to be communicated through their instructional pedagogies. These pedagogies kept with the engaged, discovery-oriented learning styles so conducive to theatrical study, but sought to strike a balance between structured and more organic expression. Though most faculty valued modeling and mentoring relationships, they perceived their instruction and personal motivations to be of greater significance and influence for faith integration among the student population. *Thus the essence of how faculty perceive the integration of faith and learning is that it is an instructional enterprise with multiple available pedagogies, driven by predominantly internal or future-directed motivations that seek to graduate students who are both professionally and spiritually mature. Relationships form through this instructional process, but they are not necessarily part of the faith integration process.*

## To What End?

This chapter has led to the development of four "essence" statements, statements that sought to capture the heart and common, shared ideals or perceptions of both the student and the faculty populations. For the students, these statements were:

- *The essence of what was imagined and how it was imagined was that a deep-seated, spiritual, and tri-directional connectivity between students, faculty, and God would occur through professional and personal relationship building, brought about through shared motivations, right preparation, and trust-based relationships where mentoring and modeling could occur.*
- *The essence of what students perceive to be effective integration of faith and learning is a supportive, networked web of methodologies, relationships, and practices, centered around professional and spiritual modeling, that foster a greater understanding of God and of humanity.*

For the faculty they were:

- *The essence of how the ideal integration of faith and learning was imagined by faculty was that it was an organic process brought about through a desire to strike a proper balance between professional instruction and faith-based preparation for students to work in the entertainment industry. This organic process would occur through varied pedagogies, including both mentoring and modeling, and had the goal of creating a lasting connection between students, their profession, and God.*
- *The essence of how faculty perceive the integration of faith and learning is that it is an instructional enterprise with multiple available pedagogies, driven by predominantly internal or futuredirected motivations that seek to graduate students who are both professionally and spiritually mature. Relationships form through this instructional process, but they are not necessarily part of the faith integration process.*

These four statements encapsulate the "invariant structure" of what students, alumni/ae, and faculty believed about faith integration, both in their ideals and in their perceptions of how it actually occurs.

Now that this information has been presented, what is to be done with it? What suggestions or recommendations arise from what has been discovered? These suggestions, along with some reflections on the process of doing this study and a few final remarks, will close out this study in the following chapter.

# Conclusion

The conclusion of this study is fast approaching. Readers began with an all-too-brief overview of the relevant literature, waded through the description of the study, delved through two chapters of detailed data and descriptive clusters of meaning, and plumbed the depths to discover the essences of student and faculty ideals and perceptions (or, perhaps, ascended to a height that allowed for an "invariant structure" to be better viewed and understood?). And now, near the end of this journey, one must ask, What has been learned on this pilgrimage?

This final chapter will begin with a restatement of some of the discoveries that arose from this study. This will be followed by a few suggestions. These suggestions are not meant to be critical of what each group perceived, but rather are offered with the hope that they might lead both groups closer to their idealizations and to more uniform understandings of each others' needs and limitations. They are also meant to be food for thought for those faculty or administrators at other faith-based universities who are evaluating their own efforts at faith integration, or who are just starting to think about the topic. After the suggestions will be a few short reflections on the process of engaging in this study. What was done well? What would the author change if given the opportunity to go back and do it again? And what were the limitations that were discovered while engaged in this dissertation process? Finally, the chapter will conclude with some closing remarks.

## Discoveries

The first discovery of this study, though it is by no means a new finding, is that faith integration is not done solely through dedicated assignments or projects. At least in this particular theatre department, faith integration was both imagined and perceived to be incorporated into the daily theatrical instruction that students were paying to receive. Students (and faculty) who spoke of "add-on" faith integration assignments nearly always did so in the negative, with the implication that such assignments were deemed to be irrelevant and unhelpful to their spiritual and professional growth. In contrast, the assignments, projects, or experiences that were most beneficial to students' faith were those that were seamlessly enmeshed with regular instruction and work. But even these assignments were not understood by the students to be the primary method of engaging with their faith; rather, observations of how faculty spoke about, used, and thought about faith or faith integration was the number one factor in how students imagined and perceived IFL.

The second discovery that arose from the data is that students have diverse and truly integrated expectations about how faith and theatre should intersect. From the relatively small data sample in this study there were five clusters of meaning and thirteen categories within those clusters that dealt with student ideals and perceptions. While the student ideals were more heavily weighted toward the influence of faculty modeling and personal preparation through prayer and study, they were particularly perceptive about what they observed in their department: with the exception of Modeling (which was the most perceived cluster by a factor of four), all other clusters were evenly observed with positive imprints left on the students' recollections. This diverse awareness brings with it the implication that since students are looking for faith integration in all these areas, then faculty need to be consciously seeking to engage with IFL in each area as well.

The final discovery that came to light from this study, and that is supported by other studies (e.g., Sherr, Huff, and Curran), is that student and faculty relationships, particularly for theatre students within this department, are an essential part of how those students understand faith integration. Every student declared that faith integration was beneficial to their field, and though this declaration was almost always followed up with a statement that spoke to their motivation, it was usually *illustrated* by how a faculty member engaged IFL. From what the author could uncover, every student who was in an intentional mentoring relationship with a faculty member referenced it as an important factor in how they valued faith integration. Similarly, many of the student motivations were in line with what the faculty wanted the students to do or be; though there was diversity within the faculty Motivation cluster, that cluster encompassed nearly every student motivation. And of course, faculty Modeling was both perceived and imagined by students to be the central way that IFL occurred. In all of these instances, relationships between the students and the faculty were a stated or an implied part of student (and even faculty) responses: mentoring by definition requires a relationship where personal information is exchanged; the common structures of both student and faculty motivations leads to an educated speculation that students derived their motivations from what they heard faculty say in times of faithful sharing; and the modeling that students perceived implies that students spent enough time with the faculty to be able to judge faculty values, practices, and relational tendencies. Thus relationships, or connectivity with those who are in positions of leadership, were an essential part of student IFL engagement.

## Suggestions

From the data that was discovered during this research process a few suggestions come to the fore. There is some hesitation here in offering these suggestions, as it is obviously far too easy to sit in an armchair and critique an institution and its constituents from afar. The splinters in the eyes of others, to adopt a Biblical metaphor, are far easier to see, after all. But there is also a belief that these suggestions are important because they speak to the heart of what some of these same faculty were saying about how faith integration "should be," and therefore they are included here. These are not meant to be critical of the efforts of the faculty, or to imply that what they are or have been doing is "wrong." Rather, these recommendations are given with the hope that they provide the impetus for expanded conversations and intentional action, both within the particular department that so graciously allowed access for this study and in theatre departments across the country. Whether these faculty take the advice that is given here is irrelevant, so long as it leads to more intentional engagement with faith integration.

From the data that was gathered, two central facts were clear from student responses: (1) students had a *very* high perception of faculty modeling as an important part of IFL, and (2) they had a much more holistic perception of faith integration than the faculty, where all parts of IFL were equally noted (with the exception of Modeling, which was high, not low). From the faculty data, two other facts rose to the front: (1) Instruction was always near the forefront of their perceptions of faith integration, and (2) they believed their motivations would be evident through their integration efforts. While these facts are important, and neither group is "wrong" in their perceptions and/or approach, there does seem to be a kind of "speaking past" each other, or at the very least a lack of awareness about how the other sees and thinks of faith integration.

Thus I would suggest that faculty, since they bear the brunt of the expectations regarding IFL, develop a very intentional and purposeful departmental plan regarding faith integration efforts. Though there were references within the faculty interviews to discussions about faith integration, the author got the impression that these were few, or that they were directed at venting frustrations about university expectations. Thus, simply having intentional, positive conversations about the topic would be a great step. And with a stated intention to develop a departmental plan, the conversation would have an end goal.

These efforts and conversations could be directed toward the creation or enhancement of a faith integration "web." This web could be designed so that each faculty member could play to their strengths, but also so that each of the five clusters identified by students as ideal parts of their IFL experience could be supported. Thus, for example, one or two faculty members might be identified as "mentors," the ones that students are directed to when they need guidance. Or, every faculty member is a designated "mentor" but in different areas (e.g., performance, academic studies, spiritual matters, etc.). One faculty member could be a designated "connector," who directs students to the appropriate faculty members and keeps students informed of activities that can build relationships beyond the classroom or production experiences. Another faculty member could be the spokesperson, whose job is to clearly communicate with the students the driving purposes and motivations that propel the faculty to pursue and engage in IFL with their students. And, though *all* faculty need to have a heightened awareness of their role as a model, one or two designated faculty could hold a "workshop" where they show their peers how they foster the natural and organic IFL that so many faculty and students spoke about as being the ideal way to engage the subject. Or, because having opportunities for faculty to *witness* how their peers foster an atmosphere where faith integration thrives (instead of just hearing about it) can be very important for generating ideas and showing shared purpose, perhaps some faculty could sit in on a class that is known to have very positive responses by students to faith integration efforts. Obviously steps need to be taken that are reasonable to the demands of the faculty's time and energies, but some steps need to be taken so that student desires are met. The webbed approach to meeting these desires is just one way that this might happen, and this author feels it could be effective since it shares the responsibility among the faculty as a whole.

As for students, faculty need to communicate to them the importance of their instructional efforts in respect to faith integration. It was communicated directly by one student that faculty attitudes toward faith integration greatly affected her own outlook on it, and several other students hinted at this in the way they spoke about faculty modeling. Thus, both faculty and students should be made aware that there is a purpose for faith integration assignments, discussions, and the like, and that these efforts are not just an "add-on" to the "real" work of theatrical study, but are essential qualities of any Christian artist. This can be communicated by the faculty through the sharing of their own motivations or their own desires for how the students will approach their craft with faith once they graduate and enter into the industry. Faculty should have no qualms about continuing to use the pedagogies that are known and comfortable to them, but they should seek to consciously mesh those pedagogies with their own stories of faith, their desires for their students' faith, and how their faith informs their approach to the subject.

Closely related to this suggestion is another, which is that faculty and students need to be unified in their perceived purpose for faith integration in theatre. Achieving this unification is a multistep process, and the first step is the hardest: namely, the faculty need to be unified in their stated purpose. For the faculty population in this study, the author believes they are close. Though they phrased their desires differently, and certain members weighted their answers more toward evangelism, professional training, or discovering more about humanity, etc., the essence described in chapter five still holds true: there was *a desire to strike a proper balance between professional instruction and faith-based preparation for students to work in the entertainment industry*. But faculty need to know where each other stand and why they stand there. Not everyone needs to have the same emphasis; in fact, it is likely better that there be diversity instead of uniformity so that students can make their own discoveries about striking the proper balance. But there must be clarity of purpose and intentionality behind the emphases of each faculty member so that the goal of effective IFL can be properly sighted. As with the first suggestion, this approach creates a "web" in which students can see a wider approach to faith integration modeled by the faculty and adopt the approach that best suits their own preferences, while at the same time creating awareness of, and respect for, approaches that they might not have noticed otherwise. But first the faculty must be clear in their own methodologies and purposes. Only then, once the faculty all understand their role in departmental IFL, can the motivation and the desired expressions of IFL be properly communicated to students. And then, once the students know the purpose(s) of faith integration within their studies, they can evaluate it and begin incorporating it into their own spiritual maturation.

Though it has been stated before, the third and final suggestion is that faculty need to be more intentionally aware of the Modeling of IFL in their instruction, in their direction, and in their general interactions with students from the Department. This intentionality requires that faculty both discuss amongst themselves and self-evaluate what type of models they wish to be. Because "Identity" was a cluster that five of the six faculty identified in their own perceptions of IFL, the process of self-reflection that is necessary for a truthful analysis of Modeling should not be foreign to them. Instead, it simply needs to be turned toward this particular component of their instructional role. The clarified expressions that come from such a process can be shared with their fellow educators. The goal for such a process is that these expressions of modeling might lead to practical ways of achieving departmental and/or programmatic learning outcomes; aid the department in clarifying its purposes within the larger institution, if this has not already been done; and lead to a more holistic departmental understanding of the role each faculty member plays in the overall educational process of the students under their care.

## Reflections

This study was challenging on multiple fronts. On the one hand, this author's familiarity with educational theatre and its pedagogical practices made it a natural focus for study. On the other hand, however, there was great ambiguity in what would be discovered: would alumni/ae have vastly different experiences from current students? What clusters of meaning would arise from each group of participants? Would students and faculty be prepared for the self-reflection required for this study, or would their answers be simply trite recitations of what they had learned from others or what the university wanted to hear? And of course, would the answers be truthful and open, or guarded and circumspect?

Many of these questions were answered as the study progressed. Alumni/ae experiences were, by and large, quite similar to those of current students. The clusters of meaning came to the forefront rather clearly once the data began to fill out. Because of the nature of study that theatrical learning requires, both students and faculty were very ready and open to sharing their experiences and reflect back on their own intentions, desires, and perceptions. And there were very few instances where an interviewee seemed cautious or guarded in their responses, and those instances, which often were at the very beginning of the interview, melted away within a few minutes.

The author was fortunate that everyone who participated in the study did so of their own accord. No cajoling or begging was ever needed, and all participants seemed genuinely happy to have contributed to the research process. There was also favor to be found from the department Chair, who graciously allowed the research to happen, offered their own services (including electronic communication with the students and faculty from a departmental email address), and who supported the work at all times. All faculty agreed to participate, and though there were scheduling difficulties to overcome, the entire department faculty were able to contribute, which allowed the study to reflect the most accurate faculty data possible. And among all participants there seemed to be genuine gratitude at having their voices heard on the issue, in the hope that their experiences, observations, and insights might lead to some kind of change for the better.

Though the process of doing a qualitative study is daunting, and the data seemed vast (even in a small study such as this), there clearly was no more effective way to learn about IFL in this particular university setting than to talk with those who were engaging in it. If time and resources were not a factor it would have been interesting to sit in on classes and observe the interplay between students and faculty, to see if the descriptions matched what was observed. It would further have been interesting to witness rehearsals for different plays or musicals with different directors, and to see what data might arise from such an endeavor. But time was a limiting factor on this study, and to do these things would have required at least another semester with the department, which was impossible. Interviews allowed for an abbreviated engagement with those who shape the direction of the department (faculty and students alike), and provided consistency in the data collection.

If time were malleable, and knowledge learned from that hard teacher, Experience, could be carried back in a magic blue phone booth to the point where this study was just getting started, this author would have crafted a few different questions from those that were asked. The challenge that this study wrought was that, while it was (relatively) simple to discover what students/faculty perceived or imagined regarding IFL, it was far less clear what these groups *valued* with respect to the topic. For example, even though students spoke again and again about faculty Modeling, was that something that carried greater weight in their own understanding of faith integration than, say, personal Motivation? Was it more persuasive to get them thinking about their faith with respect to their art? Did they value it more? The answer to these questions can be given educated speculation (Yes, because faculty Modeling was so prevalent among all student responses), but cannot be stated conclusively. Thus questions about value would have been added to those already in the interviews, such as:

- What were/are the most important types of faith integrationthat you have seen or experienced while a student/teaching at this university? Why are those the most important to you?
- What is/was the best example of faith integration you'veencountered while studying/teaching here?
- In your view, what is the purpose of faith integration? (Whatvalue does it have in a theatre department?)

Questions such as these would help to better determine how students and faculty evaluate and rank (for lack of a better term) efforts at faith integration, and the various types of IFL that exist in the classroom, the rehearsal performance space, and in relationships.

**Final Thoughts**

To conclude, this study sought to discover how both faculty and students in an undergraduate theatre department at a Christian university imagined the ideal integration of faith and learning, and how they perceived it happening at the time of the study. Through an interview process that lasted several months, four current students, five alumni/ae, and six fulltime theatre department faculty members shared their perceptions and ideal imaginings of faith integration. These interviews led to data that illuminated numerous clusters of meaning, groupings of information that captured shared elements of the various responses. These clusters, which included Modeling, Mentoring, Instruction, Motivation, Preparation, Connectivity, and Identity, were then compared against each other to discover similarities and differences between the students and faculty. Finally, from these clusters arose textual and structural descriptors that led to the four "essence" statements that are necessary for any phenomenological study.

This process led to the several conclusions. First, faculty viewed both the ideal and the perception of current IFL largely through the lens of their Instruction and their personal (and assumed communal) Motivations. Second, for the students, the role of faculty as Models of faith integration was the most perceived and imagined method of IFL. Third, even with such a high regard for Modeling, students still had a far more balanced perception of IFL than their faculty counterparts, with each of the other clusters of meaning having equal representation among the participant responses. Finally, once these conclusions were arrived at, several suggestions were offered on how to better align faculty efforts and student expectations.

The hypotheses that originally drove this study, presented at the outset of chapter two, were partially correct, though the proper answers are far more nuanced. The hypothesis that this department may not be integrating faith and learning as effectively as they might think seems to be mistaken: every student spoke about the efforts of the faculty to engage in IFL, and their responses lead the author to think that their efforts have been largely effective: every student and alumni/ae believed it to be beneficial and important for their studies. The second hypothesis, however, proved to be largely correct: faculty did not seem to be fully aware of how IFL was most acutely perceived by their students (the influence of their Modeling was largely ignored in faculty answers). The final hypothesis, that faculty Mentoring and Modeling would be most important in students' understanding of faith integration, was half correct: while Mentoring was no more important than any other identified cluster, faculty Modeling was indeed understood to be the greatest perceived and ideal way for IFL to occur.

While this particular study is finished, it is the hope of the author that it will lead to many more attempts at better understanding faith integration in the arts. Through such efforts, and the application of their findings, both future professional and lay artists might be more effectively trained to engage their faith every time they engage their art. It is the fervent prayer of the author that we never again hear contemporary stories of professional artists like John Cochran entering into a church sanctuary with the expectation of meeting God through theatre, only to be disappointed. Instead, through the intentional training of Christian theatre artists to engage their faith in their artistic endeavors, may God be encountered in every locale and incarnated in every practice.

# Appendix
## Interview Questions

1. For the record, what is your legal name, academic major, and year in school?

2. Which university or college do you attend?

3. Do you consider yourself to be a "person of faith"? What does that mean to you?

4. Do you believe faith integration is beneficial to your field or craft? If yes, how so?

5. Faculty: How do you envision or imagine faith integration happening in your classes? Students: if you were a professor, how would you integrate faith and theatre in a class?

6. Faculty: How do you envision or imagine faith integration happening in your production experiences?

   Students: If you were a professor, how would you integrate faith and theatre in a production you were in charge of?

7. Describe if your decision to come to a Christian university was related to your decision to enter theatre.

8. Describe an example of faith integration occurring in a class you've taken/ taught for your major. What other examples can you offer?

9. Describe an example of faith integration occurring in a theatre production that you've been a part of. What other examples can you offer?

10. Please finish this sentence: A professor who integrates faith and learning would never...?

11. Please finish this sentence: A professor who cares about my/a student's spiritual growth would never...?

12. Students Only: Using a scale of 1 to 10, I want you to select and rank three professors based on your perceptions of their efforts to integrate faith and learning in the classroom. Without using their names or any identifying information, please describe how you arrived at the value for each professor.

13. How have you changed spiritually during your time here at ____? Do you think your experience as a Theatre student/professor has had any impact on that change? Can you give an example?

14. Do you think your professors/co-workers within your department are interested or concerned with your faith? If yes, how do you know?

15. Are there classes you would like to see added to your/the major that address elements of faith integration or spiritual growth? If yes, what might those classes be, or what might they cover?

# Bibliography

Anderson, Ray. *The Shape of Practical Theology*. Downers Grove, IL: Intervarsity Press, 2001.

Andrews, Alan, ed. *The Kingdom Life: A Practical Theology of Discipleship and Spiritual Formation*. Colorado Springs: NavPress, 2010.

Averbeck, Bruno B., and Brad Duchaine. "Integration of Social and Utilitarian Factors in Decision Making." *Emotion* 9.5 (2009): 599–608.

Baxter, Kay M. *Contemporary Theatre and the Christian Faith*. New York: Abingdon Press, 1964.

Berger, Fredericka. "Spiritual Formation Through Drama." *ARTS Journal* 15.1 (2003): 34–45.

Boyd, Charles Arthur. *Worship in Drama: A Manual of Methods and Materials for Young People and their Leaders*. Philadelphia: Judson Press, 1924.

Brook, Peter. *The Empty Space*. New York, NY: Viking Penguin, Inc., 1988.

Brown, Jeanette Perkins. *The Storyteller in Religious Education*. Boston: Pilgrim Press, 1951.

Carnicke, Sharon M. *Stanislavsky in Focus*. London: Harwood Academic Publishers, 2003.

Cassoti, Mathieu, Olivier Houdé, Marianne Habib, Nicolas Poirel, Ania Aïte, and Sylvain Moutier. "Positive Emotional Context Eliminates the Framing Effect in Decision-Making." *Emotion* 12.5 (2012): 926–931.

Cawthon, Dan. "The Genesian Effect: Performing *Damien* Deepens an Actor's Faith." *Catholic Theatre and Drama: Critical Essays*, 208–12. Edited by Kevin J. Wetmore, Jr. Jefferson, NC: McFarland & Company, Inc., Publishers, 2010.

Childers, Jana. *Performing the Word: Preaching as Theatre*. Nashville: Abingdon Press, 1998.

Craigo-Snell, Shannon. *The Empty Church: Theatre, Theology and Bodily Hope*. Oxford: Oxford University Press, 2014.

_____. "Command Performance: Rethinking Performance Interpretation in the Context of *Divine Discourse*." *Modern Theology* 16.4 (2000): 475–94.

Creswell, John W. *Qualitative Inquiry & Research Design: Choosing Among Five Approaches*. Second edition. Thousand Oaks, CA: SAGE Publications, 2007.

_____. *Research Design: Qualitative, Quantitative, and Mixed Methods Approaches*. Second edition. Thousand Oaks, CA: SAGE Publications, 2003.

Eggleston, Margaret W. *Use of the Story in Religious Education*. New York: Harper & Brothers Publishers, 1936.

Estrada, Christelle L. *Telling Stories Like Jesus Did: Creative Parables for Teachers*. San Jose: Resource Publications, 1987.

Foster, Richard J. *Celebration of Discipline: The Path to Spiritual Growth*. San Francisco: Harper & Row, 1978.

Grainger, Roger. "The Faith of Actors: Implicit Religion and Acting." *Implicit Religion* 8.2 (2005): 166–77.

Greene, J. D., R. B. Sommerville, L. E. Nystrom, J. M. Darley, and J. D. Cohen. "An fMRI Investigation of Emotional Engagement in Moral Judgment." *Science* 293.5537 (2001): 2105–08.

Greenman, Jeffrey P. and George Kalantzis, eds. *Life in the Spirit: Spiritual Formation in Theological Perspective*. Downers Grove, IL: IVP Academic, 2010.

Greider, Kathleen. "Seminar in Practical Theology." Class lecture, Claremont School of Theology, Claremont, CA, September 28, 2011.

_____. "Seminar in Practical Theology." Class lecture, Claremont School of Theology, Claremont, CA, September 14, 2011.

Griggs, Patricia. *Using Storytelling in Christian Education*. Nashville: Abingdon Press, 1981.

Hennessey, Gail Skroback. *Reader's Theater Scripts: Improve Fluency, Vocabulary and Comprehension: Grades 6–8*. Huntington Beach, CA: Shell Education, 2010.

Herrmann, Jörg. "'Collide with Destiny!' Religion in the Popular Cinema of the Nineties." *International Journal of Practical Theology* 6.1 (2002): 49–63.

Jackson, Tony. *Learning Through Theatre: New Perspectives on Theatre in Education*. Second edition. New York: Routledge, 1993.

Johnson, Claudia Durst. *Church and Stage: The Theatre as Target of Religious Condemnation in 19th Century America*. Jefferson, NC: McFarland & Co., 2008.

Johnson, Todd E. and Dale Savidge. *Performing the Sacred: Theology and Theatre in Dialogue*. Grand Rapids: Baker Academic, 2009.

Johnston, Robert K. *Reel Spirituality: Theology and Film in Dialogue*. Second edition. Grand Rapids, MI: Baker Academic, 2006.

Khovacs, Ivan. "Divine Reckonings in Profane Spaces: Towards a Theological Dramaturgy for Theatre." PhD diss., University of Saint Andrews, 2007.

Krondorfer, Björn, ed. *Body and Bible: Interpreting and Experiencing Biblical Narratives*. Philadelphia: Trinity Press International, 1992.

L'Engle, Madeleine. *Walking on Water: Reflections on Faith and Art*. New York: North Point Press, 1995.

Lazarus, Joan. *Signs of Change: New Directions in Theater Education*. Chicago: University of Chicago Press, 2012.

Lingan, Edmund B. "The Alchemical Marriage of Art, Performance and Spirituality." *PAJ: A Journal of Performance and Art* 31.1 (2009): 38–43.

Lloyd, Benjamin. "Stanislavsky, Spirituality and the Problem of the Wounded Actor." *New Theater Quarterly* 22.85 (2006): 70–75.

McCurrach, Ian, and Barbara Darnley. *Special Talents, Special Needs: Drama for People with Learning Disabilities.* Philadelphia: Jessica Kingsley Publishers, 1999.

McKean, Barbara. *A Teaching Artist at Work: Theatre with Young People in Educational Settings.* Portsmouth: NH: Heinemann, 2006.

Meyer-Dinkgräfe, Daniel. *Observing Theatre: Spirituality and Subjectivity in the Performing Arts.* New York: Rodopi, 2013.

Mikels, Joseph A., Sam J. Maglio, Andrew E. Reed, and Lee J. Kaplowitz. "Should I Go With My Gut? Investigating the Benefits of Emotion- Focused Decision Making." *Emotion* 11.4 (2011): 743–753.

Miller-McLemore, Bonnie. "Practical Theology." *Encyclopedia of Religion in America.* Edited by Charles H. Lippy and Peter Williams, 1:1739–40. Thousand Oaks, CA: Congressional Quarterly Press, 2010.

_____. "The Living Human Web: Pastoral Theology at the Turn of the Century." *Through the Eyes of Women,* 9–26. Edited by Jeanne Stevenson Moessner. Minneapolis: Augsburg Fortress, 1996.

Moll, J., and R. de Oliveira-Souza. "Response to Greene: Moral Sentiments and Reason: Friends or Foes?" *Trends in Cognitive Sciences* 11.8 (2007): 323–24.

Moustakas, C. *Phenomenological Research Methods.* Thousand Oaks, CA: SAGE Publications, 1994.

Orme, William. *The Practical Works of the Rev. Richard Baxter, with a life of the author and a critical examination of his writings.* 5 volumes. London: Mills, Jowett and Mills, 1830.

Osmer, Richard. *Practical Theology: An Introduction.* Grand Rapids: Eerdmans, 2008.

Paul, John Steven. "'I Love To Tell the Story': Teaching Theater at a Church-Related College." *Teaching as an Act of Faith: Theory and Practice in Church-Related Higher Education,* 163–87. Edited by Arlin C. Migliazzo. New York: Fordham University Press, 2002.

Phillips, Sue. "Reflection on Classroom Practice: the Theater of Learning." *International Journal of Children's Spirituality* 8.1 (2003): 55–66.

Pitzele, Peter. *Scripture Windows: Towards a Practice of Bibliodrama.* Los Angeles: Torah Aura Productions, 1998.

Rogers, Frank. *Finding God in the Graffiti: Empowering Teenagers Through Stories.* Cleveland: The Pilgrim Press, 2011.

Root, Andrew. *Christopraxis: A Practical Theology of the Cross.* Minneapolis: Fortress Press, 2014.

Rugg, Rebecca Ann. "Dramaturgy as Devotion: 365 Days/365 Plays of Suzan-Lori Parks." *PAJ: A Journal of Performance and Art* 31.91 (2009): 68–79.

Saldaña, Johnny. *The Coding Manual for Qualitative Researchers.* Thousand Oaks, CA: SAGE, 2009.

Sennett, Herbert. *Religion and Dramatics: The Relationship between Christianity and the Theater Arts.* Lanham, MD: University Press of America, 1995.

Shaw, Susan M. *Storytelling in Religious Education*. Birmingham, AL: Religious Education Press, 1999.

Sherr, Michael, George Huff, and Mary Curran. "Student Perceptions of Salient Indicators of Integration of Faith and Learning (IFL): The Christian Vocation Model." *Journal of Research on Christian Education* 16.1 (2007): 15–33.

Smith, Yolanda. "The Table: Christian Education as Performative Art." *Religious Education*. 103.3 (2008): 301–05.

St. John, Edward Porter. *Stories and Story-Telling in Moral and Religious Education*. Boston: Pilgrim Press, 1910.

Swinton, John, and Harriet Mowat. *Practical Theology and Qualitative Research*. London: SCM Press, 2006.

Taylor, Philip. *Applied Theatre: Creating Transformative Encounters in the Community*. Portsmouth, NH: Heinemann, 2003.

Tirrell, Jeffrey. "Bibliodrama." In *Encyclopedia of Christian Education*, 1:147–48. Edited by George Thomas Kurian and Mark A. Lamport. Lanham, MD: Rowman and Littlefield, 2015.

Torbett, David. "'I Did Not Wash My Feet with that Woman': Using Dramatic Performance to Teach Biblical Studies." *Teaching Theology and Religion* 13.4 (2010): 307–19.

van Manen, Max. *Researching Lived Experience: Human Science for an Action Sensitive Pedagogy*. Second edition. London, ON: State University of New York Press, 1990.

Vander Lugt, Wesley. *Living Theodrama: Reimagining Theological Ethics*. Burlington, VT: Ashgate, 2014.

Vander Lugt, Wesley and Trevor Hart, eds. *Theatrical Theology: Exploration in Performing the Faith*. Eugene, OR: Cascade Books, 2014.

Vanhoozer, Kevin. *Faith Speaking Understanding: Performing the Drama of Doctrine*. Louisville, KY: Westminster John Knox Press, 2014.

von Balthasar, Hans Urs. *Theo-Drama: Theological Dramatic Theory*. 5 volumes. San Francisco: Ignatius Press, 1988.

Winston, Joe. "Drama, Spirituality and the Curriculum." *International Journal of Children's Spirituality* 7.3 (2002): 241–55.

Willard, Dallas. *In Search of Guidance: Developing a Conversational Relationship with God*. Ventura, CA: Regal Books, 1984.

_____. *The Spirit of the Disciplines: Understanding How God Changes Lives*. San Francisco: Harper and Row, 1988.

_____. *The Divine Conspiracy: Rediscovering Our Hidden Life in God*. San Francisco: Harper One, 1997.

_____. *Renovation of the Heart: Putting on the Character of Christ*. Colorado Springs: NavPress, 2002.

_____. *Knowing Christ Today: Why We Can Trust Spiritual Knowledge*. San Francisco: HarperCollins Press, 2009.

Wood, Carleton W. *The Dramatic Method in Religious Education*. New York: Abingdon Press, 1931.

Wuthnow, Robert. *Creative Spirituality: The Way of the Artist*. Berkeley: University of California Press, 2001.

# INDEX

www.ingramcontent.com/pod-product-compliance
Lightning Source LLC
Chambersburg PA
CBHW021236090426
42740CB00006B/554